They exercised t[...]
human beings have access to
this wonderful trait.

I define will as the blend of persistence and endurance.
You have this. Think about a child who wants a cookie.
How long will that child ask for a cookie? Until whoever
they are asking gives in and gives it to them. You were
that child and you still are.

By Todd Burrier

ISBN: 9781672025669

©2019 Todd Burrier

Cover design and layout: Dave Ryner

*"I'm lucky enough to
have been taught 3 Circles Living
by Todd Burrier through more than
a decade of mentorship.
This simple concept fuels each
day and is at the heart of every
important decision."*

Jason Stambaugh
Husband/Father/Entrepreneur/Sales Executive

"I learned the Three Circles concept about four years ago during a corporate training event instructed by Todd. With some additional coaching and mentoring from him I was convinced that this was the most fundamental truth for approaching life. I've implemented the strategies and techniques over these 4 years and it's made a huge impact in every area of my life. I credit this for the incredible advancement I've experienced in my career, for giving me the tools and confidence to start my own business, and the growth of my credibility in the community where I live. I cannot thank you enough for sharing this wise approach to life with me."

John Brown, Husband/Father/Grandfather/Senior Product Manager/Entrepreneur

"Todd's 3 Circle principal is the most practical approach for living a fulfilled life. Thanks for helping me find the areas in my life that I needed to focus on! I owe a lot of my success in my business and personal life by practicing Todd's principals and choosing a healthier lifestyle."

David Silverstein, Husband/Father/Business Owner

"I grew up watching the men in my life prioritize work with the misconception that by prioritizing work, they were prioritizing thier family. Within the span of three years. I lost my grandfather, great grandfather and my uncle on my Mother's side. It went from 4 generations of living Kibler men to 1, with me being the oldest. They died way too young and left me with a lot to learn on my own. I have two young boys. I am no good for them if I am exhausted, sick or no longer living. Todd's three circles method taught me that by prioritizing myself, I am actually prioritizing my family. I no longer feel selfish about making health my top priority. When my family is doing well. I am more creative, motivated, and efficient at work. This has translated into close to a decade of consistent growth for my company. By following Todd's three circles method I am thriving and you can do the same."

Zach Tomlin, Father/CEO of Tomlin Technology, Inc.

TABLE OF CONTENTS

INTRODUCTION

I can remember the moment like it was yesterday. I don't remember the exact day…just the moment. It was one of those "Aha" moments, but it my case in was more like an "Oh No" moment.

I was sitting in my home office in the spring of 1991. We were living in an old farmhouse in Edgewater, MD and my office was tucked in a back corner on the first floor well away from the traffic of the rest of the house.

I was almost two years into building my first business and things were taking off. I should have been on cloud nine, but I wasn't. I was mostly miserable. I had been working 14-16 hour days for so long I couldn't remember not working like that. It made no difference what day it was, I could be found sequestered in my secluded enclave unless I was out on an appointment or conducting a meeting.

I'm an introspective guy, as many introverts are, so I was sitting at my desk trying to figure out what the deal was. Why am I so unhappy? I'm becoming successful. Isn't success supposed to go hand in hand with happiness?

As I sat there pondering, I started to look further into my life than my business. Melanie, the amazing woman I married, and I weren't doing so well. We were constantly at odds about practically everything. At the time she was half way through her pregnancy with our soon to be born daughter Allie and spending her days doing everything with, and for, our son Brett who was almost two.

Most of the time I was resenting the fact that she wasn't happy with me, and here I am busting my butt to make a good life for us and provide for the family all the things I didn't have when I was a kid. It hadn't crossed my mind that maybe the problem wasn't Melanie. Perhaps it was me.

I also started considering my physical condition. My waistline had begun to expand a little, I was constantly dealing with nagging health issues, and I was frequently sick. I had always been slender and athletic, and well, just being real here, I didn't like feeling like I didn't look very good.

As I sat there considering these two things, my marriage and my health, my mind drifted back to a time a few years earlier when I was in banking. As a commercial real estate banker, my job had been to cultivate relationships with real estate developers in an effort to gain their business. This was actually one of the experiences in my life that drove me into the business I was building.

You see, I grew up in a lower middle-class family. In fact, we were so lower middle-class, that we may have been upper-lower class. I don't know for certain what our economic status was, I only know we didn't have much money. I was the kind of kid who constantly had to put duct-tape on the bottom of my Chuck Taylor High Tops to cover the holes, so that I didn't wear holes in my socks too.

I had an awesome mother, in that she loved me, and worked very hard to keep a roof over our heads. My father was only truly in the picture for a fraction of my childhood, and he then died of cancer when I was 18. I had two older siblings who were doing their own thing, so my primary influence was Mom.

Mom, a depression era child, was scrubbing floors at seven years old in a household that was definitely lower in economic class, in a section of Baltimore called "Pig Town." Her mindset was not about what you could become in life, it was centered on being lucky to have anything at all.

"It's a cliché that no one lays on their death bed and wishes they'd spent more time at the office. You know why that's a cliché? Because it is absolutely true."

As a result, I didn't grow up in an environment that catered to thinking big, or making a lot of money, or chasing dreams.

I'm not complaining. I had a great childhood playing Captain America with a trash can lid, throwing a tennis ball against a wall pretending to be Hall of Fame pitcher Jim Palmer, and walking in the Magothy River with a crab net, or my fishing rod. Kids don't need much to have fun in my experience, and they don't know what they don't have, because they are too busy having fun with whatever they do have.

Anyway, I never envisioned earning a lot of money or having success in business. I guess you could say I wasn't very ambitious, because I simply didn't think about it.

Then, when I was working with these real estate developers, my eyes opened to a few things. These were all people of substantial economic success in my eyes. They drove fancy cars, lived in mansions, and had high net worth. Many of them had come from nothing themselves. Getting to know them, made me realize that they were just people. They put their pants on the same way

I did. I wasn't a deep enough thinker to go farther than that and consider that they had struggles and insecurities and weaknesses, too. I just started to think that if they could succeed by working hard, maybe I could too.

That alone was a big shift in my thinking. Of course, I then had the voices in my head from my conditioning saying, "Don't be a dreamer…you'll never make it." But even so, I started to think that if I worked hard too, maybe I could be rich like them one day.

As I'm reflecting in my office the other part of their stories jumped right into my mind. The majority of these successful people, and I mean over 90% of them and that's not an exaggeration, had some other things in common too. They were either in poor health, had broken relationships (several were on their second or third marriage), or both.

This was my "Oh No!" moment. I realized that I was becoming exactly like them. I was on my way to being successful in my business and unsuccessful in the rest of my life. Well, at least when it came to my most important relationship and my health.

It's a cliché that no one lays on their death bed and wishes they'd spent more time at the office. You know why that's a cliché? Because it is absolutely true. In countless studies done with the elderly, the single most shared regret is not spending more time with the people they love or loved.

When this moment occurred for me, it was completely unacceptable. There was no way I was going to sacrifice what matters most simply for money or status. NO. WAY.

I began searching for how to not only avoid this all too common malady, but to flip the script and live a rich life where the things that matter the most, all flourish, and all work together. Ultimately it evolved into the simple platform for living that I call the 3 Circles.

As I write this, I have been living from this platform for close to 25 years and teaching it to others for the past 15 years. It has led to a pretty unique and awesome life, not just for me, but also for many others.

Like all things of value, it will take a bit of time to truly have it ingrained as a lifestyle, but once you do, you will be blown away by how your life takes shape. It doesn't mean you won't have hardships and struggles. You will always have those in your life, there is no "easy street" to a well-lived life. But, what you will gain is a bountiful life rich in the things that matter most.

Life is constantly applying pressure about who you should be, what you should have, how you should live, and too many other "shoulds" to mention. It's confusing and disheartening to be consistently "shoulded on" and can send anyone down a path of living someone else's life. Then you wake up one day 20 years down the road and wonder how you got to a place you had no desire to be.

I want you to have the best life you possibly can. A life rich with abundance in the things that matter to you most. That doesn't happen by accident. It has to be pursued on purpose. You will learn exactly what has worked for me and many others that have followed this way of living. This book will give you a roadmap for living the life you want, while pursuing and accomplishing the things that matter to you.

CHAPTER 1
What Usually Happens Without This Platform

The 3 Circles represent the three most significant priorities in modern life; health, relationships and money. This platform for living that leads to the opportunity for a high quality of life is based on getting these three priorities (circles) in the proper order of importance and then conducting your life based on this order. You may have other personal priorities, but these three are irrefutable if you want to have a fully abundant life.

How can I know this? Besides experience, it's pretty easy. For something to be labeled as a priority, it has to have importance. How do you tell if something is important other than feeling that it is? If there is a substantial negative consequence for neglecting something, then it clearly should be a priority.

Using the importance and neglect context, it's easy to see that these three are clearly major priorities whether we like it or not. If we neglect any of these three, we pay a steep price. The challenge, and why its commonplace to get this wrong, is our conditioning.

Money tends to be the driver. We live in societies where we need money to function. We don't live in a time where we self-sustain by living off of our land. Our basic necessities are purchased from others using money we derive by trading our skills/knowledge for wages in some way. Our further lifestyle desires are also gotten through these means.

The challenge lays in the messaging we receive constantly. "More is better. Bigger is better. New is better." Everywhere you turn, there is advertising and marketing making sure that you know that whatever you have isn't good enough. You have to get something better if you want to keep up.

When I was a kid, we had a television that was black and white, and got three stations clearly. It was the size of a bread box, and we had one. Just one. Can you believe that? Now televisions are four to six feet wide and they are in multiple rooms and they have vivid color and you can watch 900 stations, and also connect them to the internet and watch anything at all your heart desires.

Money is tied to status. Status makes people feel important. That they are of value.

Money is connected to power, freedom, choices, experiences, and the list goes on. It feels like it's all about money everywhere you turn. To be clear, I have no problem with money. I've had times in my life when I had no money, and I've had times when I've had plenty of money, and there is no question I like having more money much better.

The problem is when money is the priority that consumes us, no amount of it will make up for what it costs to acquire it.

It is easy to get so caught up in working hard to pay our bills and get ahead in life so we can provide for our family, that we neglect our health in the process. We are living in an age where all around us are messages of instant gratification and we are easily pulled into this. We work hard, get promoted make more money. We like that.

Our health on the other hand, doesn't pull at us the same way. If we neglect our job for any discernable length of time, we suffer the consequences quickly. Health doesn't give us the same signals. The body is very resilient.

If we don't do anything for our health today. It's not really noticeable. It is the cumulative effect of neglect over time that begins to take its toll. It's so easy to take our health for granted. Until something goes wrong.

Then the game quickly changes. Even a small health issue can temporarily wipe out our ability to make money. Consider the flu for a second. How productive are you when you have the flu?

Yeah, me neither. Now, you can't stop things like the flu or even a cold from happening to you from time to time, just remember to consider how debilitating it can be when your health is not good.

Statistically, if we don't take care of our health, we will get sick in a big way eventually, and substantially cut short our productive life, and negatively affect quality of life in general, because our health is at the center of everything we are and do.

The other area that gets hammered when money dominates our priorities are our important relationships.

Relationships require time and attention. Not things. The most important love relationships in your life are also the easiest to take for granted. I know this from the bottom of my soul because I have done it before and I have seen it so many times I can't count that high.

Fortunately, I have also seen lots of people pull up on the joy stick before they completely crashed their relationship. Just by getting this clarity I am laying out for you now. If you go an extended period of time neglecting your love relationships, guess what happens?

They blow up!

And when they blow up? You are wrecked.

You cannot think straight. Your stomach feels like a blender is stuck on high in it. You can't make decisions and you can't focus. And this is just the tip of the ice berg.

Just going through a difficult period in an important relationship will mess with your mind in a big way and dramatically impact your productivity in your work and take all the fun out of the rest of your life.

"When money is the priority that consumes us, no amount will make up for what it costs to acquire it."

And that's just a challenge period. What happens when it totally breaks?

Forgive me if this is hitting you close to home. It's likely you have already experienced this, at least once, but even if you haven't, you already know that when this happens, you would do anything…ANYTHING…to get that relationship back.

Essentially, it's the same situation as health. If you neglect your love relationship to pursue your career, and the relationship breaks, you would give all your success back in a heartbeat to get the relationship back.

So again, how much sense does that make? Why on earth would we give up something so dear to get something else that we would gladly give back?

We wouldn't. *If we knew better.* If we were aware of what we were doing.

And THAT is the point of this book and this platform. And the really cool thing?

You can actually do A LOT better in your career, have a lot more success, make a lot more money (if that's what you want), and have a lot better life, for a lot longer, by getting this in the right order.

It's true. I know. I live it and have lived it and have seen lots of other people live it too.

So now let's go to the other side of this equation and I will walk you through how this flows in the most awesome and powerful way when you proactively live from this platform.

{ *"Our health is at the center of everything we are and do."* }

CHAPTER 2
How The Platform Brings You to a Rich Life

Imagine for a minute, that there are two people of equal ability, knowledge, experience, time, opportunity, and drive. One of these people is healthy and full of energy. The other is unhealthy, and tires easily.

Who do you think is going to be more productive in general?

There is no question, that the healthy person will out-produce the unhealthy person. Certainly the unhealthy person can use medication and caffeine to extend their energy in the short run. They may be able to keep pace for a month or even a year, but sooner or later, the exertion on an unhealthy body that is being artificially powered will cause a significant crash and burn. In general, the healthy person will miss very little time at work in a year due to illness, while the unhealthy one may lose many entire days. And this is just the short run.

In the long run, we're talking about decades now, it won't even be close. In fact, there is a great statistical probability that the unhealthy person's years of productivity will be cut short, whereas the healthy person can remain productive at a high level well into their 70s and 80s should they choose (barring an unavoidable issue).

I personally know many people in their late 70s who are still being highly productive in their chosen work. Maybe you're thinking they should retire while they are still healthy and can enjoy it. But the reality is that if you enjoy what you do and you are healthy enough to do it, and you are already living in the 3 Circles way, you don't need to retire to enjoy life because you already are!

Now, let's look at a different scenario with these same two people who are relative equals. Take out the health impact for now, and put in the relationship circle.

Let's assume one of these people has an awesome relationship with the person or people they love the most, and the other has a relationship that is falling apart where there is constant strife and discord.

Again I ask you…who will be more productive?

This is another no contest.

The one with the thriving relationships will be more joyful, and more focused. They will "be" in their work when they are working. They will give off an attractive, positive vibe that others will like being around.

The other one will be distracted at the very least and wholly mentally un-present in the worst case, depending on how bad the situation is. They will be the model for "presenteeism"–when your body shows up at work, but your brain never arrives.

Their productivity will tank. They will have negative energy and give off a negative vibe. Hardly the recipe for working well with others.

Let's put the circles together and you will see the true power of this combination.

When you put health as the first circle, you are energized. You can pour yourself fully into your work for however many hours you allot and when you come home you are not dragging or exhausted.

You can then fully invest your time and attention into the people you care about – the second circle. By the way, this is the key to committing to the first circle. It's not selfish to take care of you first, it's *selfless*. You are doing it for the people you love. So you can show up better!

When you have taken care of yourself, and then consistently invest yourself into the people you love, your relationships thrive. There's not just less strife, there's a deeper sense of joy. Did I say joy instead of happiness? Yes. Absolutely. Happiness is a temporary situational kind of thing. Joy is deep. Joy is profound. Joy is a state of existence.

When you do this, in the right order, you show up in your career in an entirely unique way. You are energetic, positive, joyful, attractive, and magnetic. People will love to have you in their business and people will want to do business with you. Which automatically fills out your third circle, money. The place where this all comes together, is what I refer to as "the sweet spot."

This is the recipe for a highly successful life. A rich, full, productive life. Whatever it is you are pursuing you will have more long-term success this way.

I understand there are exceptions to the rule. You can do everything right and a relationship doesn't work out. You can do everything right and you get a major illness anyway. There are also people who don't do things this way and things seem to be just fine for them.

These are outliers. In general, you will have a much higher probability of an awesome life and career if you follow this formula. Of course, that's up to you. You are the captain of your ship.

Early in this journey to get the right things in the right order, I went through a very difficult financial period. I had made some major financial mistakes in the midst of a significant business disruption. For a few years it was tough sledding financially. I was broke, but we weren't broken. This platform of living carried me through, and made it easier to navigate the financial quagmire. Feeling physically good and having the foundation of thriving family relationships, and the support of Melanie, helped keep things in perspective. Sure, I was broke… but I was not poor.

I was rich in what mattered most and that helped keep what could have been a very dark period from consuming me. It's fairly common for financial struggles to break the back of a relationship, but when the relationship has been nurtured, it becomes the rudder that helps you get through the rough waters and into the next positive cycle. It wasn't long after this difficult period that I had a major success in a business venture. Would that opportunity have happened if the rest of life wasn't in such good standing? Knowing what I know about myself, I don't believe I would have even been able to SEE the opportunity I ended up acting on.

"When you have taken care of yourself, and then consistently invest yourself into the people you love, your relationships thrive."

To this point I've given you the very basic aspects of the 3 Circles approach to life. It's actually deeper and farther reaching if you want to really maximize your potential for an awesome life.

You see health isn't just about physical health. There are also the emotional, intellectual, and spiritual aspects as well and they play a huge role.

The relationship circle isn't just your love/family relationships. It's also your community and business relationships as well.

Money speaks to your job or business, but there are also more components to financial health, and there are things like heart-pursuits and side businesses as well.

It all flows the same way and it all circles back. Your career situation can have a negative effect on your health even if you are doing the right things health wise, and it can also impact your relationships negatively if you are unsatisfied or unfulfilled. Being proactive to have the order of things correct in general will lessen the impact if you are currently struggling in your career situation, making it easier to navigate and change.

In the pages that follow you will see all the aspects, how to make them happen for you, should you choose, and what it can all mean for you in the big picture.

Now we are going to dig deep into the first and most important circle, the health circle.

CHAPTER 3
Optimizing Your
Physical Health

I have been actively engaged in the health and wellness industry for most of my career. As a result, I have seen up close, both sides of the equation. I've seen more people than I can count not take care of themselves and then have to deal with the devastating consequences, and I've seen scads of people who took their health seriously early in their life, and now look better and function at a much higher level in their later years, than others in their age demographic.

The human body is resilient to a point. When we are younger we can go on minimal sleep for a long period of time, abuse our bodies physically, and nutritionally, and still feel okay. The challenge is that we actually aren't okay.

Most people take better care of their car or their home and yard, than they do of their body. Yet the reality is, you only get one body. If and when it breaks down, there is no way to replace it. You can get a new car. You can remodel your house or get some new landscaping for your yard. But at best, you can manage a broken-down body, and at worst, you don't get the option. Modern medicine has done a wonderful job of extending life, but not quality of life. What good is it to live longer, if there is little quality in those years?

> *"Most people take better care of their car, or their home and yard, than they do of their body."*

You probably have an example of this exact situation either in your family or close to your family. Growing up, my favorite relative was my Aunt Lil. She was a free spirit who was ahead of her time. A career woman when women weren't, she lived life on her own terms. I used to visit her as a kid and play cards and drink black cherry soda. She had a marvelous sense of humor and was always interested in whatever I was doing. When I started my first business, she was the only person in my family (not counting Melanie's side of the family) that was supportive.

When others were being critical, discouraging, or making fun of my choices, she would pull me aside and tell me not to listen to anyone else but to go after what I wanted in life. She had this wonderful spirit and sharp mind until she died in her mid-90s. The problem was that her body was broken down in her early 80s. For the last 15 years of her life, she couldn't do anything except sit in a chair. This wonderful lively spirit was trapped for 15 years in a broken body, being kept alive by modern medicine. I have never forgotten this lesson. When the body breaks you have nowhere else to go.

You have already read about the impact your health can have on your relationships and your career, but there's another aspect to consider. The monetary cost.

Living a healthier lifestyle does require some investment financially. Quality foods, gym memberships, nutritional supplements, and other things that maintain and improve health certainly cost more than cheap chemical-laden processed foods, and not going to the gym.

The real story though, is that an unhealthy lifestyle is substantially more costly in financial terms and in practical quality of life terms.

What is the cost of not being able to do the things you'd like to do? What will be the cost of future things you won't be able to do if you don't take charge of your health now?

What's that funny old saying? "If I knew I would live this long I would have taken better care of myself?"

That's really not funny when it's you or me and it's real.

The cost of health care is one of the fastest growing expenses in our lives, and the cost of a major illness is catastrophic financially. The numbers are staggering. It is simply much less expensive to invest in your health proactively.

Consider your car for a minute. If you don't regularly service it, have the oil changed, get tune-ups, check the tires and brakes, what will happen? It will break down. It will cost you much more over the long run than consistently taking care of it. Your body is the same way, only on a much more meaningful level.

My understanding and passion for maintaining my health started when I was younger. I watched my father die of cancer when I was 18 years old. At the time, my own health journey wasn't significantly affected by this. After all, I was 18 and at that age we feel bullet-proof. We don't even consider taking care of our health. We simply take it for granted.

It was when I was married and starting a family that I revisited this, and tried to figure out how I could avoid dying young from cancer. By the way, I have also lost a brother to the disease and my family tree is loaded with heart disease, diabetes, and other health concerns.

I recently had my 58th birthday as I write this and I am in better health now, than I was in my twenties. Before I began this journey, I suffered with frequent illness, allergies, and even an autoimmune issue. Like many young people, I spent years of my life tearing my body apart with drugs, alcohol and other poor lifestyle choices.

The changes I made, and have followed through my life, have blessed me in so many ways it would take a while to list them all. And anyone can take charge of their health by following the simple formula I will lay out for you.

"You can have a highly productive and enjoyable life well into your 80s and 90s if you take care of your body"

First, you have to be clear that our health care system is more like a sick care system. It's designed to help you when you are sick. We are fortunate to live in an era where we have such wonderful advancements in medicine and procedures. But these shouldn't be relied on as a means to live. They should be rarely needed and primarily to avert crisis or deal with an acute situation (again I have to point out that this is in general, obviously there are people born with health issues that require care throughout their lifetime, or who suffer events that impact the rest of their life).

Health care is really about self-care. It's about being proactive and doing some simple basic things habitually so that you rarely need a doctor.

I want you to have a successful, fulfilling, and active life for as long as possible. You can have a highly productive and enjoyable life well into your 80s and 90s if you take care of your body. And you don't have to be perfect or live without enjoying things you like either. It's about how you live generally.

To maximize this part of the health circle there are four things specifically that you have to be attentive to: Sleep, hydration, exercise, and nutrition. I'm going to give you a recipe that will help you if you simply follow it.

SLEEP

Sleep is essential. At night while we are sleeping, the processes in our body are wide awake. This is when the body can really focus on doing the work that sustains us when we are awake. Deep sleep is when our body's growth hormones go to work to build our muscle, repair our cells and tissues, fight disease and replenish our energy stores. If we aren't sleeping enough then there is a major imbalance between the tearing down of the body and the building up of the body. It is proven that lack of sleep is a contributor to many health maladies including obesity.

How much sleep do you need? According to research adults typically need 7 to 8 hours per night for optimum health (teens need 9). The surface effects of not getting enough sleep are obvious in how it affects performance and mood. When we don't get enough sleep we feel sluggish, and are less able to focus and think clearly so all aspects of life performance are going to be hindered. Mood is a no-brainer; if we don't get enough sleep we tend to be cranky and irritable, pretty obvious. The more subtle part of not sleeping enough is the overall impact on health, because like every other neglect in our lives, those negative effects build up over time.

Here are a few tips to help you get the sleep you need:

EXERCISE–exercise leads to a more fit healthy body in general, including the ability to sleep better. However, do not exercise within 3-5 hours of going to bed if you can avoid it. The ramping effect on your metabolism could impact your ability to fall asleep.

CAFFEINE–avoid caffeine in the afternoon and evening.

UNWIND BEFORE BED–avoid anything that stimulates your mind too much before bed. Television, the computer, and work are things that get your mind churning. This is the opposite of what you want to do before bed. Meditate, pray, read (nothing too exciting), breathe (deep relaxing breaths), and whatever else is relaxing for you is a good thing to do prior to bed.

ALCOHOL–avoid alcohol before bed. Alcohol causes you to sleep lightly. When you sleep lightly, your body does not release the hormones.

ENVIRONMENT–the best sleeping environment is quiet, dark, and cool.

BIOLOGICAL CLOCK–if possible try to go to sleep at roughly the same time every night. This will condition your body that this is the time that you sleep.

DON'T TRY TOO HARD–if you haven't fallen asleep within 20 minutes, don't let the anxiety of not sleeping set in. Get up for a little bit and do something relaxing and then go back to bed.

HYDRATION

Now, let's talk about hydration. If you were dropped into the desert with no supplies at all, in a short while you wouldn't be craving your favorite food, you would be on a panic search for water. Aside from oxygen, the next most important thing for life is water.

And for good reason; your body doesn't store water. It uses it continuously. The human body, as a general rule of thumb is about two-thirds water. Depending on the size of the person it could be a little more or a little less. The majority of your tissues and organs are made up of water. Muscle is about 75% water, the brain 90%, blood 83%, and bone about 20%.

• Here are some of the functions of water in your body:

• Transports nutrients and oxygen into cells

• Moisturizes the air in the lungs

• Helps with metabolism

• Protects vital organs

• Helps the organs to absorb nutrients

• Regulates body temperature

• Detoxifies the body

• Protects and moisturizes the joints

Many years ago, when I was getting serious about taking care of my health, I went to a seminar where water was a main topic. I was blown away by the information and immediately implemented it into my life. One of the biggest take-aways for me was what happens in the body when we don't get enough from a long-term health perspective. If we aren't getting enough water, the gap between what we need in our body and what we get is filled by toxins.

Knowing what I know about the health impact of toxicity in the body and how it can be the genesis for major health problems like cancer, I took this to heart and started drinking upwards of a gallon per day.

I noticed a difference almost immediately in terms of energy and hunger. It's easy to misinterpret thirst for hunger and is a common issue in weight control. Often when someone is snacking the actual thing they are trying to satisfy is thirst (of course it could also be a habit!). By the time you feel truly thirsty, you are already dehydrated.

Now, when I haven't had enough water, I can tell immediately in the way I feel because I have conditioned my body by drinking plenty each day.

Here are some tips for you about hydration:

It has to be water. Water with bubbles is okay, but juice, soft drinks, coffee, tea, beer, wine and the rest are not water. They have water in them, but in most cases they actually have as much of a dehydrating effect as a hydrating impact.

Try to drink most of your water throughout the day and stop a few hours before bed, so you don't interrupt your sleep by getting up in the middle of the night.

Get a refillable water bottle that you take with you everywhere you go. This way you will always be able to drink throughout the day, and you can monitor how much you are getting. I have a liter size glass at my desk and a liter size water bottle that goes everywhere I do.

Drink a big glass of water in the morning to set the stage and re-hydrate from the night. Your body used a lot of water while it was at work while you slept.

EXERCISE

The next component of maintaining your physical health is exercise. I know this one is a challenge for lots of people. But it doesn't have to be. I believe there are three primary issues that people struggle with. Time, perception, and having the energy to actually do it.

Time management is a common issue and this is no surprise. Modern lives are full of activities already and very few people have training in time management principles. The reality is that it does take time to exercise. I have been investing an hour per day at least six days a week for over thirty years. There are plenty of marketers and fitness gurus promoting 10 minute per day programs for exercise.

I'm not a believer in that. Certainly, any movement is better than none, but let's be real, you are going to need more than 10 minutes per day. You don't have to do what I do; you can do a lot of good in as little as thirty minutes per day, and you can multi-task this time so that it doesn't feel like extra time. It truly comes back to what is a priority. We all put our time and money into what we value. As you get clear on how important this is to everything else in life, it will be easier to allocate the time to it.

The perception issue is related to what many think exercise means. It's not running a zillion miles or lifting giant weights. It's as simple as a brisk walk. You don't have to be a gym rat to take care of your body. You just have to move on a consistent basis. Get your blood flowing and your muscles engaged. You never have to pick up a weight if you don't want to. Anyone can exercise and everyone needs to.

Having the energy to exercise is a bit of a catch twenty-two. Exercise gives you energy. But you have to have the energy to do it. So what comes first… the chicken or the egg? If you haven't been exercising, it's more important to do a few minutes to start and work your way up, than to go exhaust yourself and hate doing it.

The key thing is to make it a habit. Once you start, commit to doing it every day, and within a few weeks you will look forward to how it makes you feel, and you will begin to develop some endurance.

I started doing purposeful exercise when I was about 25, but became very dedicated a few years later. The difference in the dedication level was "why" I was exercising. At 25, I was at the beach with some friends. I had taken a desk job four months prior to that and had begun to put on a few extra pounds. One of my buddies at the time looked at me and said "Dude, you're getting fat!" That hit me right between the eyes.

The next day I started jogging. I never liked running as a form of exercising. I loved to play sports, but I had reached an age where playing sports wouldn't keep the weight down, and I didn't consider other things like drinking beer or what I was eating at the time. I ran consistently until I got the weight under control and then I was sporadic. I was driven by how I looked at the time, so if I was looking good, I wasn't running! Later, when I had a family, and I had my epiphany so to speak, I began exercising for the purpose of maintaining my health for the sake of my family…and of course, it's nice to be fit! This is when

I figured out ways to exercise that I enjoyed since I knew I was going to be doing it consistently for the rest of my life.

There are two things you have to be doing; aerobic exercise and resistance exercise. Aerobic exercise is simply continuous movement that you can do without being out of breath. Walking, jogging, running, riding a bike, kayaking – are examples of consistent repetitive movements. You should do this at least three times a week, but I suggest five days as optimal. Again, thirty minutes is all you need. This is great for your cardiovascular system and your lungs. Start small if you have to, but start.

Resistance exercise is where you challenge your muscles. It can certainly be lifting weights, but it can also be using resistance bands, or doing push-ups or other body weight exercises. For example, just sitting down in a chair and then standing back up ten times in a row will work your legs and your behind. There are many things you can do and all can be modified to suit whatever shape you are in. Start wherever you are and do whatever you can do and work up from there. And do this kind of exercise at least three days per week.

"Start wherever you are and do whatever you can do and work up from there."

If thirty minutes is all you can possibly spare, then alternate one day aerobic and one day resistance. The key thing is to create the habit. This will keep you active for a long time in your life and help keep your weight in the best range for your overall health. If you haven't been exercising at all, it's a good idea to see a physician to make sure there isn't an underlying issue that could be adversely affected by exercise.

If you would like to see my fitness regimen visit: www.Toddburrier.com/workoutregimen. And if you really want to get serious I suggest a fitness trainer.

NUTRITION
The final piece of the physical health puzzle is nutrition. Nothing else will

matter if you don't get this one right. Everything that happens in your body requires nutrients. Most everything that happens in your body uses vitamins and minerals. Enzymes work with these to make everything happen. There is so much conflicting information about how to eat and what to eat, that common sense has been completely lost.

Everywhere you turn there is some new magic pill or ultimate diet. I wouldn't blame you if you were confused. I'm going to make this easy for you.

First you have to be clear about how important this is. Over the past 60 years, most major health issues, like cancer, heart disease, diabetes, autoimmune, and asthma have been steadily increasing in occurrence. At the same time, we live in the most advanced medical age in history. How does this make sense?

Because the primary issue is not being addressed. There is a major gap between what our bodies need to function properly and the nutrients in our food.

Industrialized food, like processed food and mass animal production, is loaded with toxins and chemicals. The industrialization has compromised the nutrient value of our food. In addition, we live in environments that are full of toxins and pollutants.

Our bodies need more nutrients to deal with what we are exposed to, but we are living at a time when we are getting less and less from the food we eat. Studies have shown over and over that the people who get higher levels of nutrients in their diet, have a much greater chance of living a long active life. It's really this simple. I've been involved in the health and nutrition field for over thirty years and have seen the evidence up close.

From a food perspective, you need fats, carbohydrates, and protein, in addition to the vitamins and minerals. There are many positive and popular eating lifestyles that do a good job of guiding you in getting the right foods. Many of these have merit, such as the Mediterranean diet, ketogenic diet, paleo diet, etc. You can't go too wrong with adopting any of the health-based approaches and then modifying slightly where it makes sense for you.

When you go shopping, the outside aisles of the grocery store are where you want to buy your food. This is where you find the un-processed fresh foods. Fresh fruits and vegetables, wild-caught fish, and free-range meats are the best sources of nutritious food. Stay away from processed carbohydrates as much as possible.

I follow an eating program that is based on a low glycemic load that is excellent for supporting optimal health, high energy, and maintaining your ideal weight. If you would like to have an outline of the plan I use visit www.ToddBurrier.com/eatingplan.

I learned a long time ago that you cannot out-exercise a bad diet. The problem is what is a bad diet? I have followed many of the most health-based styles of eating over the years. At one point I became certified in the highest level of personal fitness training which included extensive material on nutrition. I ate very well in general or so I thought, in addition to my exercise routine. Yet, every few years my "ideal weight range" kept getting higher.

I am just under 6'0" tall and feel really good at about 175 pounds. My weight range was about 175-178 pounds for the first few years of my health journey. Then it became 178-180, then a few years later it became 180-183 and this continued to the point where I was in the high 180s and occasionally as high as 192. When I switched to the style of eating I have now been following for close to seven years, I dropped back to 175 within three months without changing anything else and have never had a problem since.

"Studies have shown over and over that the people who get higher levels of nutrients in their diet, have a much greater chance of living a long active life. It's really this simple."

You will also need to complement your diet with high quality nutritional supplements. Maybe you are thinking you can get all your nutrients from your food. I wish that were true, but it's simply not.

It's not my intention to provide a nutrition course here. Just some basics based on research and life experiences to get you started. The reason you need to supplement is simple. You cannot get what you need from food alone in the today's world.

Studies have shown that fruits and vegetables have half or less of the nutrients than they had thirty years ago. Most people don't get remotely the amount of fresh fruits and vegetables recommended as it is, but even if they did, it wouldn't be enough. These are the primary source of vitamins and minerals.

Statistically, developed nations are deficient or insufficient in many important nutrients. This is a direct result of the food being eaten, and is the genesis of most health issues. It's further compounded by the reliance on pharmaceutical drugs which interfere with how the body uses many nutrients.

This is why nutritional supplements are the perfect complement. They cover the shortfall in nutrients so the body can perform better.

It's important to use high quality supplements for better absorption and bioavailability. In my experience, you will find the highest quality products in the home business industry for a simple reason: these companies depend on their products producing results that are noticeable. They spend little to no money on advertising, have lower distribution costs, and don't spend money on retail space. Instead they generally put more money into ingredients which yields better products. This isn't a universal truth, but it is true more often than not.

"The bottom line is that taking care of your health is not optional if you want to have the best life possible."

When you shift your eating habits to a cleaner more natural approach and supplement with good products, you will probably notice a difference in how you feel in a relatively short period of time. You will likely be sick less often, have more energy, and find that some of your nagging health issues aren't bothering you as much.

The bottom line is that taking care of your health is not optional if you want to have the best life possible. I know this was a short course, but it is enough to be a game-changer for you.

Think about a five-year-old child. Do they need three cups of coffee a day to keep going? No. They go and go and go, and then they sleep. That can be you. When you take care of your physical health, there is a lot more living each day that you can do, for a lot longer in your life.

There are no guarantees. Some people do everything right and they still get a major illness. However, you will greatly reduce your risk for a health issue, and you will have a better chance for a long, productive life.

I'm not trying to play Doctor here for you. I'm just sharing exactly what I did that changed my health in a substantial way. At 58 I have tons of energy, am rarely sick, and take no medications. The basics I gave you in this chapter could make a huge difference for you too. If you research deeply everything I've suggested you will find the scientific validation, and if you look around you at the healthiest, most vibrant people you know, you will often find that this is similar to the blueprint they may be using.

CHAPTER 4
Optimizing The
Mental Part of
the Health Circle

I've struggled with a poor self-image most of my life, and this has been made even more challenging given my "wiring." The chemical balance in my brain is apparently a little off such that I don't know who will wake up in the morning. Borrowing from Winnie the Pooh, I wonder if it will be "Tigger Todd," the guy who is playful and energetic and sees the world as a wonderful place, or will it be "Eeyore Todd," the guy that feels like nothing is good and what's the point of getting out of bed? These two characters perfectly describe what I personally experience.

The reality for me, is that more of my mornings Eeyore is alive and well, regardless of how wonderful my life is. However, I don't use it as an excuse to roll over and stay in bed because I woke up as Eeyore. Instead, I go to significant lengths to minimize it so I can show up every day the best way possible.

Most of the people that know me are shocked when I share this part of my story. They see me as very positive and optimistic. Only those closest to me, like Melanie, know the battle I go through to show up every day. I tell you this because we all need to work with whatever raw material we've been blessed with. And I want you to know that each of us has our challenges and you are not alone in yours.

"Each of us has our challenges and you are not alone in yours"

All through my teen years I thought something was really wrong with me. Heck, I felt that way well into my thirties. My journey of personal development and self-discovery helped me to see that it's not that something is wrong with me, it's simply becoming aware of who I am and then working with that. It's my perspective, and definitely my experience, having worked with and coached many people from all walks of life, that most people feel this way.

The bigger problem is that no one talks about it so we feel like we are not normal, whatever normal is, when in fact it is a normal part of human life to be imperfect and have areas of weakness. Yet, here we are struggling silently and feeling alone in it all because everyone else, including us, is presenting this image that we have it all together.

I believe this is especially difficult for men, and more so for young men. The idea that men shouldn't show weakness or emotion seems to be alive and well in modern culture. Without the societal "permission" to be authentic and admit that we have struggles, we tend to hold these feelings in. This creates a disconnect between who we are and who we are being which is an underlying stress that not only affects us day to day, but will come out in some fashion at some point when the internal cauldron boils over.

"Manning up" so to speak is to be strong in the face of the world and is the manly brave thing to do. My newsflash for you is this…it's a lot more courageous to admit you aren't Hercules. Pretending for the sake of image…that is the cowardly act.

You have all you need to make your impact in the world and with the people in your life. The key to doing this is becoming self-aware and then actively working to improve yourself. The concept of self-awareness is to know yourself as you truly are, accept what you don't like and understand how that is actually beneficial for you, and utilize your strengths to move forward.

I'll give you an example. Anxiety is one of the things I would rather do without. That's not an option. It's part of my genetic make-up. I can proactively manage it, but it will always be there. But what's good about this aspect of me? It keeps me working at things. You see, the truth is that I love to play. I like to fish and play with my dogs and enjoy a good book, and anything else that is fun, I am automatically up for. I'm not driven by status, or titles, or awards, or big money. I simply am not wired that way. My anxiety is actually a blessing in that it keeps a sense of urgency alive in me that keeps me striving to do better. You may think I'm crazy…and in the sense that we are all a bit crazy, I accept that. But that's how I see it, and I encourage you to try to find the positive side of the things you would rather not have to deal with as well!

Self-awareness is a huge component of Emotional Intelligence (EQ). This aspect of each of us is much more responsible for our successes in life than our Intelligence Quotient (IQ). In the book "Emotional Intelligence 2.0" the authors concluded, based on their studies in the workplace, that 90% of the top performers were high in EQ as opposed to the low performers where only 20% were high in EQ. It makes perfect sense as you look further into it.

We are all emotional creatures whether we like it or not. We feel things first and then we think. There are lots of smart people who don't make much of an impact because they cannot get past their feelings. Think about someone in sales for example. The majority of people who get started in sales struggle with the emotional side right away. They don't think about the logic at all when they first start. The logic is that if you have something of value, and you present it to enough people who are open to this value, some will say yes. It's essentially a numbers game.

Instead, they have all this fear roiling around inside of them about what someone might say to them or think about them. This is emotion. Many people drop out quickly because they don't manage these emotions by recognizing them for what they are.

I bet you have had an idea about something you wanted to do or something you wanted to create and were excited about the idea. And then you started to have the feeling about the possibility of failure or rejection, and talked yourself out of it. It happens all the time. People get scared of what they don't know yet, or what they don't know how to do yet, and allow that to define the outcome before they even start!

They lack confidence. This is emotional. They forget that everything they know how to do right now, at some point they didn't know how to do! What breeds confidence? Competence. How do you get competence? You work at something, progress through the learning curve, fall down a lot, and gradually you get better and your confidence grows. It's a logical path that we have all done over and over. But if we let the emotions stop us, we never go through the learning curve and develop the confidence. Simple.

Another thing that impedes us all is comparing ourselves to others. We tend to look at other people who are successful in some area that we might want to work at. Do we see what they went through to get there? Do we see the weaknesses they had to overcome? Do we see the hardships they endured? Do we see the tears they shed? The moments they felt like they couldn't go on?

NO. We see what they look like now. And we compare our just getting started self, to their already been through it all self. Does that make sense? Absolutely not. It's just emotions getting in the way again.

You have all you need to do the thing that is in your heart to do. It's how we are designed. What's in the heart is possible when we are willing to go forward without knowing it all. You are congruent with your heart. You aren't missing anything.

BUT, you have to work at the thing and you have to work on yourself. In addition to working on the thing there are four areas that you can consider and those are what I will walk you through now. These all fall under the idea of personal development, and this will change your life and positively impact those you care about, and your work-life as much as anything else because it will be your emotional energy producer, and this is just as important, if not more, than your physical energy.

HOW ARE YOU CENTERED?

This is a powerful thing to understand and address that I first learned through the late Stephen Covey's groundbreaking book "The Seven Habits of Highly Effective People." Your center is your source of security, guidance, wisdom, and power. It drives your decision making, because you naturally make an effort to satisfy it.

"You have all you need to do the thing that is in your heart to do."

Covey broke it down to nine typical centers: spouse, family, money, work, possessions, pleasure, friend/enemy, church, and self.

All of these present our source of motivation and self-worth, and we react to life based on these. You can read the book to get the deeper context of these (and I encourage you to do so), but for our purposes, the point of these nine is that they are very limiting.

We have all been, and still are affected by, being centered in a few of these. At different points in my life I have been money, work, pleasure, self, and friends/enemy centered. And the outcomes in those periods were not very good.

The ultimate centering is to be Principle-centered. This is purposeful, and serves all corners of your life. It creates the ideal mental environment in which to live. It allows you to step back from your emotions and filter whatever the situation is through a set of pre-determined values and principles. This makes decisions simpler, and minimizes the likelihood of making them from an emotional place, which you definitely want to avoid. It is never a good idea to make a decision when you are too emotionally high or low.

This is a proactive approach to life that allows you to feel more confident in what you do and yields predictable results over time. I encourage you to take some time and write down what your personal tenets are and then use them as guideposts.

Here are a few of mine:

• Treat others with kindness and respect

• Be honest

• Serve others as a means to advance self

• Everything is a process

• Live the three circles in the right order

• Everyone is here to contribute and everyone has value

• Things of meaning take time and consistency

• Err on the side of over-giving, over-communicating, and over-caring

• Never sacrifice the long term for a short- term gain

• Under-promise and over-deliver

These aren't all of them, but a pretty good start. Take the time and make your list and then do your best to live each day by them and they will make a difference. It won't always be easy, but it will be worth it.

MENTAL STANCE

In Hal Urban's book "The 20 Greatest Life Lessons" he talks about a Harvard Research study that showed that attitude is 85% of success and ability is only 15%. This goes hand in hand with the statistics on emotional intelligence.

There is no doubt in my mind that this is true. When you look at successful people, there are way more differences than commonalities. There is one thing they all share and that is will. They simply refused to quit. That is an attitude thing, not a talent thing.

I have always been a slow starter in practically everything. I've never had an IQ test, but I would guess that my IQ would fall in the average range. The thing that has led to my successes in life, has been my refusal to quit. I am referring to my adult after age 28 life of course, prior to that the ONLY thing I didn't quit was school. High school because they make it pretty easy to graduate if you just show up enough, and college because it was so much fun I did just enough to stay!

We've all met people who have achieved and thought to ourselves "that person made it?"

Yes. Because they exercised their will. All human beings have access to this wonderful trait. I define will as the blend of persistence and endurance. You have this. Think about a child who wants a cookie. How long will that child ask for a cookie? Until whoever they are asking gives in and gives it to them. You were that child and you still are.

We don't grow out of things. We grow on top of them. We all have access to the five-year old in us who sees the world as unlimited in possibility. We just have to reach down inside and grab hold.

"Your attitude impacts everyone you touch in addition to your own potential in life."

In general, how do you see things? Do you see the proverbial glass as half empty or half full? This is not a little question. It's a story-teller.

We will tend to get what we expect. If we expect little that's what we get. If we expect much, that is also what we will get. Why is this true?

It determines our mental stance which will drive our actions.

In the years of my life where I gave into my poor expectations I got little. Every time I pursued something I would eventually quit. Looking back through the lens of maturity and self-development it's quite easy to see how that happened.

Everything of value in life is going to require struggle as we grow and strive. If your expectations are low, that it can't work out for you, then you see the struggle as a sign it won't work, which leads you to stop and prove yourself right. The person with the right expectations doesn't see the struggle this way. They see it as a sign that they are on the right track. They know there will be difficulty and they know that through will, they will get through it eventually. It is the expectation that drives the decision to keep going, and that is entirely a result of their attitude, or mental stance.

This is just as true with relationships as it is with pursuits. How do we over-turn the glass? How do we pour out the contents and confidently know we can fill it back up again?

Through a process of working on our mental stance consistently.

First you have to acknowledge how you got to the half-empty perspective in the first place. You have been conditioned to think negatively.

Social psychologists, through tons of research, have determined that the average person hears some aspect of negative about themselves 150,000 times by the age of 17. "No you can't," "You won't," "You're not enough," and just plain old "no," in addition to a litany of other discouraging remarks. On the other side of the coin, you hear something positive 5,000 times. That's a 30 to 1 ratio. Is it any wonder 85% of the population suffers from low self-esteem?

You know those two little characters that sit on your shoulders? The one with the black hat who's always negative and the one with the white hat that is the one who says you can do it? Thanks to the constant conditioning you've had the black hat on one shoulder has become Goliath compared to the little white hatted David on the other shoulder!

In addition to this, we are surrounded by negativity. The media apparently believes its job is to dramatically sensationalize every negative thing possible. They polarize us and terrorize us all day long. Fear is their drug. It's all around us all the time.

You can't give into this. You have to actively work at balancing it out because the impact on your life is just too big.

It's hard to completely eliminate the negative, because you have the condi-tioning of a lifetime and the constant bombardment daily. You can reduce the effect though, and over time see the good and cultivate a positive frame of mind (after all David won and so can you).

It's a crucial part of the health circle because your attitude impacts everyone you touch in addition to your own potential in life.

I will provide three key strategies you can employ to help you out.

All of these strategies are focused on growing your self-belief. This is the attitude driver. What you believe determines your choices, which determine your actions, which determine your results. If the belief platform is faulty, everything else will be too.

A belief is simply a thought that you continue to think. That doesn't guarantee it's true. For centuries people thought the world was flat. Was that true? Your world isn't flat either.

PERSONAL SUCCESSES

First, let's tackle the issue of what you are capable of. The world has done a pretty good job of conditioning you to think "not much." I bet that if I asked you to tell me about some of your failures or mistakes or disappointments, you could readily provide me a list. You have been programmed to build monuments to these as indicators of what you cannot do.

If, on the other hand, I said make me a list of all your successes, this would be a tiny list.

Yet, in reality, this list is substantially bigger than your failure list. The only likely exception to this are serial entrepreneurs, because their key to success has been to fail as often as possible until they figure out what works. There's a very valuable lesson in that. Don't let fear of failure keep you from trying things. The failed attempts are part of the process. They only become true failure when you quit trying.

Anyway, the point I'm making is that there are so many things you now do easily, comfortably, and/or very well, that at some point you didn't know how to do at all. These are called successes. You are only reading this because you successfully learned how to read. How long did that take? Quite a few years didn't it?

You can walk, drive, write, manage your life, speak a language and maybe another one, and the list goes on for a long time. It's easy to only point to some recognizable achievement as a success, but that is a faulty view. Those are good. I enjoyed being the 5th grade math flash card champion, but just learning math was a success too.

What's the point of this? It's proof. Proof that whatever you dedicate yourself to you eventually do successfully if you don't stop working at it.

You might not remember learning how to walk, but I assure you that was one of the hardest things you ever did. Most other things in life are a lot easier on you than that was. How many times did you fall down? Hit your head? Face plant on the steps? Yes, this is a little tongue in cheek, but it's a true validator of your will and the fact that you can do most anything you put your mind and heart into.

Understanding this is empowering and it takes the lid off of life, and it is tremendously valuable in shifting your attitude for the better.

I often will have a coaching client who is struggling with their self-belief create a success list and it's extremely insightful for them.

This would be suggestion number one for you. Since it's not my place to tell you what you SHOULD do, I can only encourage you to do it. Make a success list. On this list include everything you have learned how to do, in addition to all your accomplishments, achievements, victories, and awards. You will be blown away by the size of this list. You might find you're pretty good after all!

GRATITUDE

Strategy number two would be utilize gratitude as an attitude booster. It is virtually impossible to be thankful and negative at the same time.

We just aren't wired that way.

It's been proven in study after study, that those who cultivate an attitude of gratitude are happier. It makes sense when you consider the thankful versus negative thing.

Here's a crazy question for you…

Have you ever considered how great it is to have a big toe? What would it be like if you didn't have one? It would be very difficult to walk, you certainly couldn't run, and just standing still would take quite a lot of effort.

My sister has a plaque in her home that says "Imagine how you would feel if you lost everything you had right now. And then got it all back."

That's a powerful thing to consider. Just thinking about it brings a massive sense of relief doesn't it? Why don't we feel that way every day? I believe it's because we are often focused much more on what we DON'T have as opposed to what we do.

I'm not suggesting you shouldn't try to achieve more, acquire more, become more, and experience more. I am not a fan of complacency. I think that leads down a dark road. We aren't very happy in life when we stay stuck in any particular place too long. We become restless and bored. We are better off continuing to strive to become more. And be careful to not confuse complacency with being content. A good friend pointed this out recently. Contentment is a sense of satisfaction and a bit of happiness in where you are, which is an excellent heart place to work forward from.

When you stop for a few moments to ponder all that you have to be grateful for, this also is a big list. It affords you the ability to push away feelings of lack which are attitude killers.

In fact, barring an extreme issue like a terminal illness, your life is so rich in things to be grateful for, regardless of your current perspective on this, that there are truly billions of people in the world who would change places with you in a heart-beat.

You likely have an abundance of food, shelter, skills, resources of some kind, people in your life that love you, access to a bounty of activities, services, and entertainment, and the list goes on.

Here are two more suggestions for you. The first is to make a gratitude list. Consider everything you could possibly be glad you have or have access to. If you need more clues, look at this exercise inversely. Think of everything you would not like have taken away, from your personal freedoms to anything physical to relationships and possessions.

Making this list will reveal just how abundant your life really is. Life is pretty good when you have abundance. Once you make this list, revisit it daily for a little while.

The second idea for you is to be purposeful throughout the day to recognize things you are grateful for. Throughout your day there are so many things to enjoy that are all around you. Nature, people, and experiences are abundant daily if you take the few seconds to acknowledge them.

This cultivation of your gratitude will have a direct effect on giving you a positive outlook.

STRENGTHS

The third and final piece to this mental stance component is your strengths.

Once again, due to our conditioning it's important to take the time to assess these, because these are how you make your way in life and make the contribution that only you can make.

We can easily point out our weaknesses. These are the things we either aren't wired for, or haven't taken the time to develop. Like you, I have many. I am not very good with details, not very handy, not very technical, not very good at organizing things, not very strategic, easily distracted, socially awkward, and the list goes on. So what?

No one is good at all things. That's how it's supposed to be. It's how we complement each other in life. Your weaknesses don't define you or limit you, unless you choose it.

The key is simply to manage weaknesses. In most cases it's not even necessary to work on them, with one exception. When it interferes with your ability to use a strength, and only you can do it (particularly in business).

"Your weaknesses don't define you or limit you, unless you choose it."

It's much more valuable for you to identify your strengths and then work on them. You can magnify a strength because it is how you are built. There are many things that can be considered strengths. From a practical perspective, your resources, knowledge, skills, and network of relationships, are all strengths.

From a more personal standpoint, you can easily identify areas that represent potential strengths by paying attention to a few things. I learned this years ago from Marcus Buckingham's book "Go Put Your Strengths to Work", and it helped me considerably to begin to see myself and others in a different light.

Consider these four questions:

What are you good at?

What kinds of things do you learn quickly?

What things are of true interest to you and you feel drawn to?

What things, when you do them, give you energy, make you feel good, and time seems to fly?

Answering these four questions will reveal strength zones for you. When you are operating in your strengths, these are the times you feel like you are in a zone. You feel like you can just go and go, and you do so confidently.

Uncovering your strengths gives you another glimpse into what's good about you. This helps you feel better about yourself and your potential, and will have a foundational effect on improving your attitude.

I encourage you to take some time and list all of the strengths you can find, both personal and practical, and then consider how you can apply them in your life and work.

Before we leave this topic, I mentioned earlier that you have to manage your weaknesses. If you don't they can make you feel overwhelmed and frustrated, and these are not good things for your attitude or your productivity.

Here are some tips for managing a weakness.

Sometimes a weakness is simply something you haven't taken the time to learn. It's possible this is because it's not in your strength zone, so you haven't had the interest in doing so, and it's also possible it is in a strength zone but you are just now being exposed to it.

If it is affecting your ability to use your strength's effectively, and it isn't something you can have someone else do for you, then you have little choice but to learn it enough to be adequate. Which you can. There are two personal examples for me that may help you understand what I mean.

When I started my first business, I had to talk to people about what I had to offer. Making the initial contact to do this is not in a strength zone as it flies directly in the face of my introversion. Since this was not something I could have someone else do for me at the time, I had to work extra hard at this to mitigate it as a weakness so that I could get into my strength zone, which is the actual conversation.

The second area for me had to do with my non-technical inclination. There are certain things, like making videos, doing a blog, etc. that I had to learn how to do. It was, and still is, painful for me, but I learned enough to function. I can drive someplace one time and naturally remember how to get back to that place. I can perform a technical function on a computer 50 times and still not readily remember how I did it. This is a perfect example of what it can be like learning in an area of true weakness. I'm never going to be super good with technology. It just doesn't interest me enough and it drains me to work at it. That's how a weakness is readily visible. Fortunately, there are several other strategies that you and I can employ.

The converse of this previous example is teaching. Years ago, through building my first business I discovered that I love to teach. It just fills me up to help others this way. I can teach all day long, and at no point during the day do I feel tired. That's because it's a strength zone for me. Now I may be completely fried an hour after I finish because I pour myself completely into and it takes a massive amount of emotional energy, especially since my teaching style is interactive and all-in, but never during.

It's a clear natural strength. I've had times where I traveled abroad and conducted intense training/teaching sessions for 10-12 consecutive days in different cities. Each day required hours of travel, a minimum of 4-6 hours of teaching, several hours of social interaction (which drains me), and minimal sleep. Never during these trips, and I have done several in my career, have I been at all fatigued when I am in that teaching moment. This is the power of operating in a strength.

There are five things that you can do to keep a weakness from impacting you so much:

USE SYSTEMS—Many things can be systematized such that you simply paint by numbers and don't have to think about it too much.

DELEGATE—There are many things both in your work and in your personal life that you can have someone else do.

CONTRACT—You can hire someone to do the thing you aren't good at or takes away time from using your strength more.

COLLABORATE—You can work with someone else on something where you are in a strength zone and they complement you by doing the thing you are weak in and they are strong in.

INNOVATE - You may be able to creatively come up with a way to move past the weakness.

This wraps up this piece on attitude. By taking the time to do the three things – Success List, Gratitude List, Strengths Assessment - you will make a noticeable and positive impact on your mental stance in life as you realize your glass is always pretty full.

One last nugget here that relates to your personality preferences. It is extremely valuable to invest a little time and money in taking some sort of assessment. A DISC profile, Meyer-Briggs, and there are several others, can go a long way to helping you understand a lot about yourself. These kinds of assessments provide insights into your personal tendencies and preferences, are excellent self-awareness tools, and allow you to see yourself objectively so you can better work on you.

There are three other areas that contribute to optimizing the mental component of the health circle that further strengthen you: Intellectual Health, Spiritual Health, and your attitude about change which my bride calls "Silver Linings." I'll touch on them briefly for you.

INTELLECTUAL HEALTH

Intellectual health, in my way of thinking, has little to do with your IQ, and everything to do with learning and keeping your brain active.

I've heard it said that knowledge is power. That's incomplete. Knowledge *put into action* is power. The more knowledge you have in any given area, the more confident you are in taking action in that area.

Make an effort to study and learn about the parts of your life that matter to you. If you want to do better in your relationships learn more about people. (In addition to what you learn here) If you want to do better in your industry learn more about it. If you want to be healthier, learn more about that.

Learning is good for your brain. It loves to learn. The more you know about something and put what you know into action, the more you will naturally do these things without having to think about it, which allows you to learn more.

The other thing that is good for your intellectual health is to constantly challenge your brain.

You have creative energy that is waiting to be tapped into. You have to nurture this. Games and puzzles of all kinds are excellent for keeping your brain engaged, active, and healthy.

Reading, listening to educational material, watching educational videos, and spending time with people who challenge your thinking are incredibly valuable to your intellectual health. Try to do these things as often as possible.

SPIRITUAL HEALTH

This is a deep topic and I'm not an expert here, but suffice it to say that people who are actively engaged in their spiritual well-being tend to be more grounded, peaceful, and considerate of the welfare of others.

It's not my place to tell you what you should believe or not. That's personal. What I am suggesting is that whatever spiritual journey you are on, be purposeful in making room for this in your daily life.

I follow the Christian faith. For me, that's not just showing up in church once a week. It's a daily thing. I read from the Bible most every day of my life. It doesn't make me better or worse than anyone else. I make more mistakes in my life than I like to admit and I'm sure you could find some measure of hypocrisy in me frequently.

That's called being human. We should all be respectful of what others' believe. I know I used the word should there, but in this case, that's pretty accurate. I'm not respectful of people who intentionally hurt others who don't believe as they do, but I am respectful in everyone's right to believe what they believe.

I read and study people based on the value they provide. I couldn't care less what their religion or spiritual beliefs are. Everyone can teach you something.

The point is, that this area is a component of your overall health circle and it's important to keep it active in your life if it is important to you.

FINDING SILVER LININGS

As we conclude this section on the mental part of the health circle, there is one last thing I want to remind you of and it has to do with change.

We live in a world that is changing rapidly. Since technology builds on itself, change is happening all around us faster than ever and the pace of change will continue to increase.

Human beings are made a little uncomfortable by change. We get the apples arranged in our life's cart just the way we like them, and then something happens to upset that apple cart. Change means a step into the unknown. Because of our negative conditioning, we often see change as negative on the surface. It brings out fear.

This is true of change we make on purpose, and it's definitely true of change that happens to us without our initiating it.

The first thing to recognize is that a change is not good or bad in and of itself. It's not possible to know the true meaning of a change in your life, because it ultimately affects many other things going forward.

Every decision you have ever made has represented some level of change and has impacted many of your future decisions. This may not be true of deciding whether to eat fish or chicken for dinner, but when it comes to life decisions it is absolutely true.

You are exactly where you are in your life as a result of all the change you have embraced or resisted in the past, in addition of course, to your habits.

"Big silver linings typically arise from very difficult changes."

Melanie and I were kayaking one evening when she said the words "silver linings" about something we recently went through. This is what inspired me to include this topic right now.

We had recently made the choice to change where we live. It was a huge decision that would affect the rest of our lives. We had spent the past 25 years in Westminster, MD. We loved the area, the people, and were well established in the community. The only thing missing for us in Westminster was water.

We both love being on the water. Since we both work from home, and our income isn't tied to one geographic location, we could have moved to the water many years ago. We chose not to uproot our children during their school years, and then once they had moved on to their own lives we began seriously looking into moving.

To make a long story short, we purchased a home on a beautiful river in North Carolina, and four days before we were scheduled to move in, a major hurricane did substantial damage to our property, setting off an incredibly difficult period that lasted several months.

This meant we had two massive changes to work through at the same time. The one we chose, which was to move in the first place, and the one we didn't which was to have our entire plan turned on its head.

To say it was difficult would be a giant understatement. Yet, many good things have come from the situation, hence the concept of silver linings.

If you were to look back on your life at many of the changes that you didn't wish were happening when they did, you would find that there was usually something really good that came as a result.

If you can keep this in mind as you navigate difficult changes, it will help you stay positive despite the struggle. I know it's not easy to do in the midst of struggle, but it helps to sustain you through doing what you need to do, especially when you don't think you can go on.

33 years ago, as I write this, I had a job that I was excelling in. The company ran into a problem and overnight I had no job. As a result of that, I ended up going back to bartending in the short term to pay my bills. I needed an income immediately so I reached out to a friend who was working in a nightclub an hour from my apartment. I ended up getting a job as a bartender in that nightclub, and the second night I worked, I met a beautiful waitress that I have now been married to for over 30 years.

I met the love of my life because of a massive unexpected change.

A few years later, the same thing happened to me when I was a commercial real estate banker. The job went away overnight, and ultimately, I started my first business that completely changed the course of my life for the better.

Big silver linings typically arise from very difficult changes. There have been several of these in my life, and I bet there are many in yours. It would be a good idea to reflect on some of those, to help you be positive in embracing changes in your life as you go forward, and help you be open to new things.

CHAPTER 5
Cultivating The Love Relationship Circle

The next circle in the flow is the Love Relationship circle. Everything you learned in the Health circle, put into action, will put you in the proper head and heart space to invest in this important circle.

Taking care of yourself provides the physical and emotional energy to show up the right way for the people you love. As I mentioned earlier, relationships require time and attention, and little else. No amount of material possessions will take the place of this.

If you think back to some of the happiest times in your love relationships, you will find that it was often times when you had very little in the way of money or things, but you had each other. And that was more than enough.

One of the things that most of us human beings do over time, is begin to take things for granted. We forget how important some things are when they are always there. That's one of the powerful things about the gratitude list. It reminds us of how thankful we are to have what we have, and few things need this kind of appreciation like our love relationships.

When you invest yourself in these relationships, you don't just have happiness. You have joy. Remember, joy is a much deeper emotion that trickles into everything you do.

In this chapter you'll get a variety of tips and insights into how to best take care of these supremely valuable relationships.

KINDNESS, HONESTY, AND RESPECT

These three basic tenets are behavioral platforms in your personal life as well as in your business. Keeping these in the forefront of your mind during every interaction is vital.

Kindness speaks for itself. Treat the people you love with kindness as much as you possibly can. This isn't always easy, because it's easy to have our emotions become charged, and given the closeness of the relationship, it is also easy to let your guard down and be unkind at times. When you behave unkindly, apologize as quickly as you can.

Honesty is not optional either. There are always going to be times when the truth hurts. But it will never hurt as much as not telling the truth will eventually. Honesty builds trust which is at the center of all your relationships. The deeper the trust the deeper the relationship. Trust needs to be protected like the precious jewel that it is.

Put these together and you have the essence of a powerful proverb:

"What is desired in a man is kindness; and a poor man is better than a liar."- Proverbs 19:22

When you make a mistake. Own the mistake.

Respect is essential for maintaining harmony. You will constantly have differences of opinion on things with those you love. They have as much right to their opinion as you do to yours. You don't always have to agree on everything, but you do have to respect the other person's opinion.

When I teach conflict management, we begin with clarifying how conflict starts. It begins with a difference of opinion. Is this a conflict? Not really. It may be conflicting opinions but it only escalates into conflict when there is a lack of respect.

"If you think back to some of the happiest times in your love relationships, you will find that it was often times when you had very little in the way of money or things, but you had each other. And that was more than enough."

Lack of respect is the mother of all conflict. It is better to simply agree to disagree in a kind, loving way.

WALLS AROUND TIME

This isn't going to be easy at first, but I suggest you treat some aspect of your time with your family as if it was a scheduled appointment that can't be changed or interrupted. This is natural in business, but not so natural in our relationships.

It's so easy to let the outside world jump in to this precious time. When I first became aware of how my imbalance was affecting my marriage, I actually blocked the time in my schedule to just be with my family in general and with Melanie specifically.

Your relationship circle is more important than anything else in life outside of your health, and it has to be consistently worked on daily. There will be occurrences in life when other things might need all your attention for a window of time. A special project in your work, or some type of crisis in life, can throw you out of balance for a period of time, and make it virtually impossible to be in relationship mode every day.

This is a normal part of life and easily navigated when your basic mode of operation is to show up consistently otherwise.

Here are some simple ideas that will make a big difference if followed consistently:

• Have a specific time in each day when you have uninterrupted time with the people you love, that is other than having a meal together. In this time together, turn off the TV, shut down the computer, and put your phone out of reach.

• Have a date night each week. It doesn't matter what the date is, just that it's sacred time together.

• Once a quarter try to get away for a long weekend together.

• Once a year go away for a week together.

Time is the crucial element here. Not what you are doing.

I know that when you have children, especially small children, this is more difficult. The time with the children is essential too, so do similar things with your children. Some parents make their cars a no phone zone so they can use their commuting time to school and practices to interact with their kids. Simple game nights or story time is another way to connect.

Something I recognized when my children were young was that when they had something to tell me or show me, the moment was fleeting. I remember experiencing the disappointment on their little faces when I would say I was too busy. What was I busy doing? I don't remember. That's how truly important it was. I did however, remember how it felt to see the look on their face as they walked away. I'm so grateful I figured this out quickly. When they were still really little, like 3 and 5, 90% of the time, when they would excitedly come to tell me or show me something, I would stop everything in that moment and give them my full attention.

If you think about it, what do you have going on when you are home that is more important than your child knowing you love them and care about them? If you have small children or plan to in the future, here's the truth. They are NOT convenient. They are not sensitive to what you have going on in your life. They don't care about the checkbook or your promotion at work. They just want your attention. My relationship with my children is incredible, and it all started when they were little. When you don't take the time to be in the moments that matter to them, you cannot get those moments back. They will move on to the next thing. And if you continue to find everything else more worthy of your attention, i.e. your phone, computer, television, etc. eventually they will stop coming to you.

BE THERE

We just covered the time part, so now it's time to address the attention aspect. There is so much going on in life it's easy to be physically present but have your mind be a million miles away. When you are with the people you love, it's important to be fully present.

The way you can make sure this happens is to focus fully on them. Try to remember that the person in front of you right in this moment is more important than anything else you could be doing in the world.

"When you take the time to truly listen to someone, it is likely you are the only person to offer this kindness in that day."

Listening is an emotional investment in the people you love. It demonstrates that you deeply care. This is a lot more important than you may realize.

We live in the most connected time in human history. Everyone has a phone in their hand with the constant ability to be in communication with others, and with the social networks they are part of. As a result, we are also in the most distracted time in history. There is simply an overwhelming amount of competition for our attention.

When you take the time to truly listen to someone, it is likely you are the only person to offer this kindness in that day. It's easiest to tune out those we love. We are around them all the time.

We can assume they know we love them. But this doesn't work. It has been measured through scientific research that feeling ignored has a tremendous impact on a human being. It is just too easy to be so busy doing things that we forget to stop and BE with the people that matter most.

The people you care about need your validation that they matter. Listening to them makes this happen.

This hurts even now to share but I hope it helps you. In the early days of our marriage, before my "awakening," frequently I would be in the kitchen with Melanie and she would be talking to me, sharing something about her day, or her struggles, or her life, or you name it, and I would literally just turn around and walk right out of the room without even acknowledging that she was speaking. That's how un-present I was.

She would say things to me about it from time to time, but I just brushed it off, because I wasn't really listening to her then either. I know now, and have for many years how painful this must have been for her and how alone she must have felt. There are always going to be times when you are miles away in your mind due to something happening in life, but this needs to be the exception. I am so grateful she loved me enough to stay with me while I was such an idiot, because she certainly would have been justified in walking away. I was lucky. Don't bank on luck. Pay attention to the people you love the most.

Put your phone down, turn away from your computer, turn off the TV, and be with them.

Listening is an essential skill for the rest of the relationships in your life as well, and this includes the people in your community and those you interact with in business.

CONSIDERATION

Being considerate is another way to demonstrate that someone matters to you. No act of consideration is too small to be meaningful.

Little considerations are things like spontaneously doing something for someone that they don't expect. For example, maybe you are out doing something and you see something you know your partner in life likes. Maybe they collect glass turtles and you happen to see one. You buy it and give it to them just because you know they like it. It's a little thing, but it is "the thought that counts."

If you are sitting together in your living room and you get up to get something for yourself from the refrigerator, it's as simple as saying, "Can I get you anything?"

It's saying "please" when you ask them for something and "thank you" when they do it. It seems so little, yet it means much.

It is so easy to lose sight of this. I have been reminded more times than I care to admit, in times when I have forgotten these little considerations.

Larger considerations have to do with commitments you make. These are larger life issues that impact your time and resources. Before you say yes to things, stop and think, how does this impact the people I care about?

About seven years into our marriage I was presented a business opportunity that felt right to me but the timing couldn't have been tougher for the family. We were in a very difficult financial situation. Between the income I was earning in a business that was limping along, and what Melanie was bringing in working part time in a restaurant, we were barely keeping up with our bills. We had discussed that it was time to make a change for several months as my heart was clearly not in what I was doing, and that is not a recipe for growing something, so it was obvious my present business wasn't going to be the answer.

After fully investigating the new opportunity, I knew that given our circumstances, the only way it would be plausible to pursue would be to immerse myself for the first 90 days. I could not in good conscience make that commitment on my own, because it represented a risk to the family in general, and it would have a substantial impact on the entire family in the short run since I would be essentially absent.

Rather than just doing it, Mel and I spoke about it. I shared my perspective on it, my belief that it felt like the right fit for me, as well as my concerns and the reality that it might not work out. After discussing it she asked me "what do you think you should do?" I told her that I believed that in order to do what was necessary to make a go of it and to create enough income to bridge the transition, I would need to fully immerse myself for the next three months. She supported the idea, and thus I made the commitment.

Had she not agreed at the time, I would not have made that commitment. I would have looked for something else as a primary means and likely pursued the opportunity as a side gig. It would not have been considerate to just move forward full force without her blessing because in essence, my commitment represented a commitment for her as well in that she would be doing much more of the heavy lifting for the rest of our family life together, in addition to working.

If you are concerned about the impact on your loved ones, discuss it with them. Sit down and say, "Here is something I am thinking about doing, but before I make a decision, I wanted to run it past you."

Do these things take time? Yes, they do. Are they worth the time it takes? No. They are worth A LOT more than the time it takes.

ASSUME POSITIVE INTENTION

It's natural to judge someone's actions and not their intention, while at the same time we judge our own intentions instead of our actions.

We are all going to consistently make mistakes and errors in judgement. When it comes to the people you love, try to assume positive intention. Especially when it comes to things that hurt your feelings.

Think for a minute...Would the person who loves you purposefully try to hurt you? Possible, but not likely.

Why do pencils have erasers? Because people make mistakes. No one is perfect. Ever.

Since we all make mistakes, it's important to be forgiving of those we love when they make a mistake too. If the mistake affects you or hurts you, assume it was unintentional and ask what they were thinking when they did this. You might consider starting the question with something like this:

"When you did (fill in the blank) it hurt me. I know you wouldn't do that on purpose, can you help me understand what you intended?"

SUPPORT

There will be times when the people you love have a desire to do something that you either don't understand or don't agree with. Perhaps they want to make a career change, or start a new business, or go on a trip they've always wanted to take.

It is crucial that you are supportive of their desires and goals and dreams. If you are unsupportive to the degree that they don't do the thing that is on their heart to do, this is a recipe for future problems because it will breed resentment.

Resentment is a nasty thing and has a deep and lasting effect on a relationship. There's nothing wrong with being a caring voice of reason. Asking questions out of love, to help them be clear about all that may be involved, is smart and helpful.

However, playing "devil's advocate" for the sake of trying to be right, will be wrong for you in the long run, even if you are right.

Instead, come from a place of support and encouragement. Ask how you can help them make it happen. Ask them what they need from you. Ask them how you can best support them.

The heart is a powerful thing. If someone you love has a heart to do something, the last thing you want to be is negative.

FORGET THE SCORE

There are things you bring to the relationship, and things you do for the relationship and vice versa for your life partner. It is natural to look at what you bring as important and valuable. It's also natural for you to be acutely aware of every little thing you do.

On the flip side of the equation, it's natural for you to not realize all that they are doing, and how important it might be to you and your relationship with them.

"Give as much to the relationship as you can and let things play out from there."

Keeping score just isn't appropriate and will never be accurate. A classic manifestation of this would be when one person is the primary breadwinner and the other takes care of the household. It is so easy for the breadwinner to look at their role as more important (I could be speaking from prior experience!) and keep a mental tab running.

This is a mistake. Running a household, especially one with children in it, is a major job that many breadwinners would struggle to do. If you don't believe me, and this applies to you, try taking over for a few weeks and see how it works out for you!

Instead of thinking about who is doing what, just do all that you can do. Give as much to the relationship as you can and let things play out from there.

BE GRATEFUL

I know I brought this up in the prior chapter, but that was for your attitude. This is taking it to an entire new level. You are blessed beyond measure to have people that love you and that you love. There is nothing better on the planet.

You get to have a life with these people. They are the people who will be there for you when no one else will be. These are the people you can truly trust. The people who will pick you up when you fall.

The people who defend you, support you, and cherish you. The people who don't care how you look, what you wear, what you drive, or what your job title is.

These are the people who know you the best and love you for who you are. Remember this as often as you can.

This is something to be immensely grateful for every day of your life.

When you consistently show up for these people, and invest yourself in them, you can experience true joy in your life.

Maybe you haven't been doing so hot in this area so far. That's okay. Today is a new day. Tell them that you love them and then show them that you mean it by being there completely.

Things will turn around quickly, and it will have a far-reaching impact on everything else you do.

You will show up in your work in a more positive and energized way, and everywhere you go, people will be touched by the light you bring.

CHAPTER 6
Community and Business Relationships

"When you need a friend it's too late to make one." I'm not certain where I heard this but it is spot on for this chapter. In general, people do business with people, not companies.

Certainly, there are things that we buy where this is not as much of a consideration, especially when it comes to online purchases or groceries, hardware, and other commodities of this nature. Having said that, when there is a problem, how you are treated by the human being you interact with, will have a major effect on whether or not you continue to patronize a particular company regardless of what it is you are buying.

As a general rule though, relationships drive business. You cannot simply call on someone only when you need something. You have to invest in the relationship. People do business with those they like and trust.

If you think about the people you do business with, the people whose services you consistently employ, the shops you consistently go into, even the place where you get your coffee, you will see that there are people that you enjoy interacting with and that you trust to do a good job.

We live in a world where there are more choices than ever. In essence everything is a commodity. For many of the things you choose, price is not the driver, the relationship is. Loyalty is only with people, nothing else.

I know there are exceptions. There are one-time things, or immediate needs, where the relationship is not considered. That is not the point here, everything I teach is to serve you in the long term of life.

When you are attentive to your own well-being, and to your most important relationships, you show up extremely well in the business world and in your community, because you are energetic and convey a joyful spirit, which is magnetic.

THINK OF COMMUNITY AND BUSINESS AS INSEPARABLE

Every interaction you have in your community has a long-term effect on your reputation, which directly impacts your credibility. Credibility is the driver of all your opportunities with people and in business.

You never know who is watching you. You have no idea who the person in front of you or behind you is in the grocery line, or who they are associated with. You have to be consistently the same nice, honest, and respectful person both in work and outside of your work.

I observe people all the time in public settings. I like to watch how someone interacts with the server at a restaurant, or the sales clerk behind the counter at a store. When I see someone treat someone in service poorly, I believe I am seeing the true person.

Have you ever seen someone be unkind to someone in a setting like this? What did you think about them? Did it make you want to get to know them? What if you observed someone behaving badly towards another person, speaking unkindly and being condescending towards them, and then later that week you had an appointment only to discover that the person who would like to do business with you was the unkind person you saw mistreating another. Would you be able to brush that off since in this new situation they were putting their best foot forward and treating you well?

"Everyone wants to be recognized and feel like they matter."

No. You wouldn't. You would be seeing their prior behavior. You wouldn't be able to trust that they were being genuine with you. This speaks to the power of honesty. Integrity is a wholeness. You want to be around people you can trust as being true.

When you are nice to people everywhere you go, it makes a difference. It's noticeable. It's easy, yet, it seems to be difficult for a lot of folks.

Everywhere you go, smile and acknowledge what someone is doing. Everyone wants to be recognized and feel like they matter. The next time you are in a store or at the gas station, smile and say something nice to the person who is helping you. It will make a difference for them. This little tiny gesture on your part will brighten their day and they will remember it.

This is also a sign of respect. Not one person in this world is any better than another. Different, yes. Better? No.

Everyone has value and everyone has a story. You can learn from anyone and everyone. Never judge someone based on what they wear, what they drive, what house they live in, what they do for a living, or anything else for that matter.

George Washington Carver said "How far you go in life depends on your being tender with the young, compassionate with the aged, sympathetic with the striving, and tolerant of the weak and strong. Because someday in your life you will have been all of these."

In my eyes, this is about respect and compassion. Respect everyone, unless they are specifically trying to harm you or others. Never forget Maya Angelou's famous words "People will forget the things you do, and people will forget the things you say. But people will never forget how you made them feel."

SERVING, GIVING, AND SPONTANEOUS OPPORTUNITIES

There are five things I write in my planner almost every day of my life (They are also part of the daily recipe I use to overcome "Eeyore Todd" on those mornings where he is alive and well!):

• Who will I impact today?

• Who will I serve today?

• What will I learn today?

• What cool things will happen today?

• Who will I thank today?

These five things frame how I approach a day. The impact and serve questions are relevant for this section. Every time you are nice to someone you make an impact. Every time you help someone for no reason aside from the fact that you are in a position to, you serve them and also make an impact.

Think of it like this, you have spontaneous opportunities daily to give and serve and you have more structured, planned opportunities.

The questions I write, help me to be aware of the spontaneous opportunities. If you go to the grocery store and you see someone elderly with a cart full of groceries, take a minute and help them put the bags in their car. So simple and easy for you, yet so impactful for the other person.

Do it because it's the right thing to do, not because someone could be watching. But understand someone could be watching, and it will make an impact on whoever is.

I was on a phone call several years ago with a man named Bob talking about some business. I don't remember the topic of our conversation, just that at one point he said to me in the conversation, "Do you know when I knew you were a person I could trust?" I had no idea what he was talking about. At this point I had known Bob for about ten years. He said it was a long time ago when I was speaking at a large event in Atlantic City. He knew of me and we had met, but we really didn't know each other at the time. He told me that during one of the breaks at this conference he came around a corner in the lobby, which was empty except for me and a woman in a wheelchair that I was helping into the elevator. He told me that since there was no one else around, he knew I was doing this from my heart, and not as a display for anyone else. This single thing that I didn't remember, cemented his belief in me as a person. That is a powerful lesson that I have never forgotten.

You never know who is watching when you do something helpful, perhaps no one is. But you will know you did it, and the other person will be grateful.

> "One of the best ways to lift your own spirits in life is to do something for someone else."

One of the best ways to lift your own spirits in life is to do something for someone else, and every day you have opportunities to do this. Think about the first part of that sentence for a second. I know the only time I really feel bad mentally or emotionally is when I am focused on me. What I'm not, what I don't have, what I'm not accomplishing, all the noise that plays in my head is focused on me. When we focus on serving someone else, that noise goes away.

From a purposeful standpoint there is an abundance of opportunities to give and serve in your community. If you have the financial resources, then make sure you are giving to others who are trying to help themselves or who are in need.

If you are not flush with money, then give your time and your talents. I'm not very handy, but I can do grunt work. I can pick up trash, lend my back to a project, or lend my teaching skills to someone who needs it.

What can you do? Look for opportunities to be involved and serve. It's the right thing to do, and it will have an impact in your business life as well.

You will meet other people of the same spirit. You will make new connections and further your reputation as a good person. Even though you are doing this out of the spirit of giving, not getting, the universe has a way of paying you back, and you will find doors that open up to you as a result.

LISTEN UP

People gravitate to those that make them feel valued and who they believe care about them. In fact, the pathway for others to receive input from you on practically anything starts here. It's about trust. If people feel you have their interests at heart, and that you truly care, they will trust you.

The next step on that path is for them to feel that you understand them. Once someone is trusting of you, and believes you truly understand them, then that is the point when your input has merit for them and will be considered. This applies to business as much as it does personal relationships.

The key to having someone feel understood is listening. I mentioned earlier that when you listen to someone, you are likely the only person to do so in that day, but it's possible you're the only one to do this in the past week. Or maybe even longer!

This is the single most important relationship skill there is. Yet, very few people have any real training on this essential skill. I have an MBA. When you think about all the years of schooling that degree required, it adds up to 18. In those 18 years, at no point was I required to take a course on listening. We learn lots of things that help us to become employable through school, but we don't learn the very skills that allow us to be highly effective with people or with our personal productivity. This is why this is a fundamental area I teach in most of the training sessions I offer for corporations.

Hearing is a gift, but the ability to effectively listen has to be cultivated and practiced. Even when we know exactly how to do it well, it's still difficult. Physically we can process 450 words per minute. Yet, the average person speaks no faster than 150 words per minute. This leaves a lot of room for our minds to wander. We can be hearing and processing every word someone says, while at the same time be thinking about what we want to eat for dinner.

When we are purposefully listening, we use this extra space in our processing ability to see the other aspects of what someone is communicating. It has been well researched and documented that only a small part of what someone is communicating is coming from the words they are saying. The rest come from the nuances of their body language, facial expressions, tone of voice, and pace of speaking. These are what is communicating the emotion. This is the key to true understanding.

In addition to this physical barrier, we have several other barriers to listening that can range from prior experience with the person speaking, to hygiene, personal space, distractions in the environment, how we are physically feeling, and the list goes on.

The biggest barrier we have is our lens in the discussion. Often we listen auto-biographically. This means we are processing based on what we think about what is being said, or our motivations in the conversation. This is where things like judging and assumptions get in the way. This is the wrong way to listen because it is about us. We need to focus fully on the other person.

To help you work on your listening skills, I'm going to give you a simple 3 Step formula you can practice, that will quickly make a noticeable difference with the people you interact with.

STEP 1: FOCUS COMPLETELY ON THE OTHER PERSON–When they are speaking make them the entire universe. Nothing else matters in this moment but them. Forget completely about you and what you think or care about or know. It's not relevant at the moment. Let them feel the intensity of your focus. As I said earlier, all that extra space left in your brain between your 450 word hearing capacity and their 150 word speaking capacity is available for a reason. And it's not to think about dinner. It's to be attentive to the other more important aspects of what someone is saying; their feelings about what they are saying.

Pay attention to all the nuances of their expressions in their face and how they are gesturing and behaving physically. Pay attention to their tone and pitch and the speed in which they talk and notice when it changes. Work at feeling them. Have you ever heard someone say "I feel you?" when you tell them something? They probably didn't. It was just something cool to say, but this is actually what you want to be doing. This is the big stuff. This is where the deeper connection can happen, because when you ascertain some-one's feelings, you have created an emotional tether and trust grows quickly.

When you are listening with this kind of purpose, your physical presence will mirror this. The technical practice of listening is to use appropriate facial expressions, soft eye contact, open body language, and congruent acknowledgers, like "uh-huh" at the right time. But you don't need to even consider this part when you listen this intently, because you will naturally do these things.

STEP 2: ASK AN OPEN-ENDED CLARIFYING QUESTION–Remember this is all about understanding them. So, it's not important yet, that you have some brilliant perspective to share. They want to be heard, not enlightened… yet. They may want your wisdom at some point, but only once they are truly feeling understood.

A clarifying question is one which reveals context and meaning. These are the most powerful questions in interpersonal communication. They can be in the form of an open-ended question, which allows the other person to freely expand and go deeper, or they can be in the form of a closed-ended question which serves to affirm that you are getting what they are saying completely. My favorite open-ended clarifying question is "What do you mean by that?" Which you could also say as "What do you mean when you say….?" This question closes the gap that naturally occurs when two people are communicating. It eliminates the potential for you to respond based on assumption.

"Assumption is the mother of all miscommunication."

Assumption is the mother of all miscommunication. You say one thing and I hear another. It's natural since we are all different and have our own unique perspectives and experiences. When you ask an open-ended clarifier, this gives them the freedom to explain in a different way if necessary and wipe out the potential to be fooled by what you think they are saying.

More importantly, this question demonstrates that you are truly attempting to understand them. It doesn't even matter at this point if you get it or not, it matters that they know you are trying! You are instantly making them feel valued. You are displaying a true investment of your attention.

At this point they will either, share a little more insight, and you will have clarity, or they will say essentially the same thing again using different words, and you will know exactly what they are saying, and be ready to move to the next step.

STEP 3: PARAPHRASE–This is where you let them know that you really understand them fully. In this step you use a closed-ended clarifying question (closed-ended questions are questions that lead to a specific response, such as yes, no, one, two, blue, green, etc.). My favorite one is "Are you saying… ?" You finish this question by paraphrasing what they just said in your own words. When you do this, one of two things will happen. First, you understood them correctly and they will say "yes." The other option is that you didn't understand them, and they will say some form of "no."

If they say yes, you can now respond or ask a new question if you would like to continue the conversation thread and have them talk.

"People are drawn to those who encourage them."

If they say no, then simply ask them to help you understand what they really mean. They will love this. After all, who takes time nowadays to really try to understand what you are saying? You simply go through the process again until you get to the "yes" for the third step.

This little three step formula is easy to do, and will make a massive difference in the impact you have when communicating with others. People will walk away from a conversation with you feeling very good. And they will remember this.

ENCOURAGE AND SUPPORT

Everyone you touch cares about something and is trying to accomplish something. One of the best things you can do is be a supportive and encouraging voice into this person's life. Just like you, most people hear discouraging comments on a regular basis. Hearing encouragement from someone is so rare that it is memorable, but more importantly, it is tremendously valuable.

John Maxwell calls encouragement "the oxygen of the soul." It helps to breathe life into the efforts of others. It helps them to believe that they can do the thing they are trying to do. People are drawn to those who encourage them.

Encourage with specific acknowledgement of why you believe they can do it. Let them know the traits and strengths you see in them that you believe will allow them to succeed. Then offer your support.

Ask them if there is anything you can do to help. It could be that there is someone you can introduce them to. It could be that you can be a sounding board for their plan. Perhaps you can offer some advice based on your experience.

Your support should come from a place of serving them in their pursuit first, as opposed to being hired by them to do some work. This certainly could happen, but be supportive from a giving mentality, focusing on how they could succeed. There have been more times than I can count where I had a cup of coffee with someone who was trying to build a new business or considering a new direction.

I helped them however I could without financial compensation. It was a way I could serve, I learned a lot in the process, and in many cases, it led to opportunities for me later, even though that wasn't the motivation.

The proverb says "He who waters will himself be watered" (Prov. 11:25). Think of encouragement and support a little like watering someone and helping them grow.

People will always remember those who encourage and support them.

NETWORKING

As a natural introvert, networking does not come easily for me. I'm a bit socially awkward generally and uncomfortable in settings with lots of people I don't know. Having said that, I still network, because it is a smart thing to do and it is important to continue to expand your contacts.

Join your local chamber of commerce, or other groups/clubs where you can meet people. Then make a purposeful effort to go to the events whenever you can. Even if you are uncomfortable like me, it isn't hard to meet people and cultivate new relationships and contacts.

The key to effectively networking is focusing on the other person. Everyone else who attends these events is also looking to expand their potential to do business. This makes it very simple for you. All you have to do is ask people about what they do and then let them talk. The more you listen attentively and the more questions you ask, the more the other person will enjoy talking with you. Recognize that most people's favorite topic is themselves and what they are interested in. By engaging this way, you will learn a lot about the other person, and they will think you are the greatest conversationalist they ever met...even though you aren't actually saying much!

This will help you identify the people that resonate with you, as well as people you would like to develop as business relationships. It's quite easy to reach back out to someone you meet this way and invite them to coffee to explore synergies and commonalities.

"The key to effectively networking is focusing on the other person."

You only need to take a few business cards with you. At each event make it a goal to have a meaningful connection with a few people. The worst thing you can do is be what is called a networking "mongrel." You have met these before. A mongrel is a person who goes to a networking event and invests no time in a contact. All they do is essentially say hi, and give you a business card and try to get yours.

I had an experience not long ago where I was at an event, and was speaking to a friend who is also a great reciprocal business contact. He introduced me to someone who immediately whipped out a business card and handed it to me. Then told me all about what he did. I never even had a chance to ask him. He just launched into it. He never asked me a single thing about myself. After he walked away, my friend looked horrified, turned to me and said "I am so sorry man, I had no idea he would do something like that." I left the card on the table.

Each person you meet think to yourself, "How can I help this person do more business?" If you have this mentality, you will quickly get to know people and cultivate an excellent reputation as someone people want to be connected to.

A FEW OTHER TIPS FOR NETWORKING:

• You will likely have some sort of beverage in your hand. Hold it in your left hand so that when you shake hands, your right hand won't be cold and damp.

• When you meet someone look them directly in the eyes, smile, and shake their hand firmly, with a few pumps of the hand.

• Say hello and nice to meet you. Then ask them what kind of work they do. After they tell you, ask them how they got into that line of work. Ask them how long they have been doing it. Ask them what they love about it. Ask them if they grew up in the area. Ask them who their ideal client is. Ask them if they live in the area. These are all easy conversation starters and allow the other person to expand.

• If they have a big job title or own a business, a great question to ask is how they came to be in that position. This opens the door for them to tell you their story which will bring many other things into the conversation, such as family, life changes, and personal interests.

• Ask for their business card.

• Once you have established some connection, follow up the next day with a text or email and let them know how much you enjoyed meeting them and that you look forward to the next time you meet.

• The door will now be open for you to reach out.

Learning how to effectively network will help you to create a level of rapport which is the beginning of trust. The key thing for getting to know people and them getting to know you is consistency. Keep showing up and treating people well, and your credibility with the people will grow, affording you opportunities.

CHAPTER 7
Optimizing the Money Circle

Why are you doing whatever it is that you are doing to earn your income? Is it because it's lucrative and you like to have a lot of money? Is it because you truly enjoy the people you work with? Do you love the specific job or profession? Is it fulfilling and in line with your sense of purpose?

So often people are in a career and they have no real understanding of why. Yet, this very thing is at the center of how you will show up every day. Once you have the Health Circle and the Relationship Circle in the right order and are consistently being in those circles, it is a game-changer for the Money Circle.

Whatever career you are in, implementing 3 Circles Living will put you in a better position to advance, and allow you to make a bigger impact day to day. I threw you the why question, because if you are in a career you do not enjoy, or that's not a good fit, this is going to become very obvious to you as you move through this chapter.

You see, when you are having challenges in the Health and/or Relationship Circles, it's difficult to truly know whether or not you are in the right work. You already have so much weighing on you outside of work, that your job can seem better than it is, because it's a reprieve from your life away from work. It can also seem worse than it really is, because you are in such a bad place personally that it's hard to compartmentalize what is what and everything just feels wrong.

It's my belief that the majority of the people working in a job are not happy in that job. Many studies say the number is as high as 70% of employees are not happy in their work. My years of working with people from various backgrounds and careers supports this belief, but the "why" of the problem is all over the map depending on what the study is focused on proving. It can be lack of compensation, lack of feeling appreciated, lack of support, few benefits, mind numbing job activities, difficult work environments, lack of fulfillment, and other things that make work a sad place to be.

Since you are the focus of this book, this short chapter is designed to help you with three things:

• To develop clarity that you are doing the right work for you,

• To help you excel in the work you do, and

• To increase the opportunities for advancement in your work.

ARE YOU DOING THE RIGHT WORK?

There're two simple things you can look at to help you confirm if you are in the right job or business for you; how you feel about going into work and how you feel when you leave.

Let's start with how you feel about going to work. Do you have a sense of dread or do you have a sense of peace and positive anticipation? Since we all have to work at something and earn an income, this question sets aside the likelihood that you would rather be doing something else besides working. Even though I absolutely love the things I do to earn a living, I would rather fish, go crabbing, or spend time with my family than work. I'm just being real here. Yet, most days, I get up and work. I have a choice and so do you.

We exercise choice all the time, and we tend to do it based on the perceived consequences of not doing something versus the perceived benefits of doing something else.

It's natural to not always feel like going to work. The deeper question is that after you set aside the desire to play or do things you really enjoy, do you not like going to work? If the answer is yes, then it's vital that you unpack why this is, so you can address it.

We all have an innate need to feel that we matter. That there is a reason for our existing. Since we spend roughly 25% of our life working, it stands to reason that it is necessary to feel like our showing up every day is meaningful in some way, and not just to receive a paycheck. We can earn money in countless ways, so it needs to be about more than money. When we are doing work that we know has meaning, where we know we are making a difference, and is in an area that resonates with our values, then we can experience a great deal of fulfillment.

Many people don't realize how important their job actually is. This is very true at the lower levels of a business, and it's unfortunate. There are no unimportant jobs by definition. If a job exists it is because it provides value to the success of the company. And any company that succeeds is doing so because they are adding value in some way to peoples' lives, yet often the employees don't really know how that is happening, or how what they are doing is contributing to that.

Think about an entrepreneur that starts a small business. Let's say they open a coffee shop. When they first open that shop, typically they have invested a large amount of their assets. They may have mortgaged their home or put most of their life savings into the venture.

At first, they aren't just making and serving coffee. They are also doing the accounting, ordering, marketing, and being the janitor. They are doing everything that needs to be done to make the business run and provide a positive customer experience.

At some point they hire someone to do some of these things. They take a new risk when they hire someone, but they do this because all of these things have to be done. Let's say that the person they hire is responsible for doing the cleaning. How important do you think it is for that coffee shop to have a clean restroom?

If you go into a place that handles food or drink and the restroom is dirty, how does that make you feel about consuming anything that is made there? On the other side of the coin, if you go into an establishment and the restroom is spotless, doesn't that give you more comfort in being there?

Now, do you think the person cleaning that restroom realizes how important this is? They have a huge impact on the profit potential of that business, and they likely have no idea.

Whatever it is you are doing has value. If you don't know how your job impacts the company, ask someone to help you have clarity. Let's suppose you are cognizant of the importance of your job but you still dread it? The next thing to look at is how is the environment in your job?

Is it a positive place to work? Do you feel respected and valued by the people you work for? Do they invest in developing you? If the answer is no, then this presents you with something to proactively address. You can do your part by bringing your healthy, happy self to work and being a positive influence, but if the environment does not reciprocate this, then it may be time to consider looking elsewhere.

The third thing to consider here is the actual work you are doing. Does it utilize your strengths? If it doesn't then you are going struggle to be highly productive and this will make you feel bad about the work. Earlier, I gave you a recipe for looking at your strengths. This would be a good time to revisit this exercise in the frame of your job. If you aren't using your strengths enough, you will not enjoy your work. It's possible that you are in the right place, with the right people, but you're doing the wrong work for your skillset. If this is the case, talk to your employer and express that you want to make a better contribution and feel you would be a better fit in different role.

The other thing to consider is how fulfilled you feel in the work you do. If you are in a great environment, using your strengths, recognize how important your work is, and still aren't looking forward to going to work, then it's likely you are not feeling fulfilled by your work.

Fulfillment is the deeper sense of satisfaction from what you do that is typically tied to purpose and meaning, and very personal in nature. It could be that the resulting impact of the work, although of value to people, doesn't resonate deeply with you, or it could be that you simply don't fully understand the impact. Either way, if fulfillment is a key thing for you, it's important for you to do work that touches you this way.

> *"If you aren't using your strengths enough, you will not enjoy your work."*

The whole idea of fulfillment is something that I was late to the party discovering. It's only been in the past 15 years that I recognized how important this is for me, and then began making decisions based on this as a parameter. Learning is so easy when we look backwards isn't it? I can see now, how it finally dawned on me. What I discovered is that while there are two clear journeys in our accomplishment evolution (achieving and transformation) there is a third silent journey paralleling these two as we go through life, and that is the values evolution journey.

My values journey in business began in earnest with freedom, then it moved to family, and then it moved to serving others through teaching (training, coaching, mentoring). These values, in my experience, build on one another. I fell in love with teaching because it felt good to do it and was in my strength zone. But as I got grayer in the beard, I realized it was because helping other people do better in life fills me up, i.e., it is completely fulfilling. The act of teaching is fun, but the true impact on a life…that is immensely fulfilling.

Everything I do in business is driven by fulfilment at this point in my life (help-ing others to achieve a richer life). I frequently turn down lucrative opportunities because they do not fit this for me, and on more than one occasion I've changed directions on something based on achieving more fulfillment. I look at this as being heart-centered. When you do what is fulfilling it is generally in line with where your heart really is. Others may not understand it, and how could they? They aren't privy to what's in your heart or what fulfills you.

If there is one piece of advice I would give to a young person, aside from living according to the 3 Circles, it would be search for what is fulfilling for you to do (follow your heart), and in doing that, you will more than likely have your financial needs met sufficiently, and if not, you will happily do something on the side to continue doing the thing that fulfills you.

Whatever matters most to you, whether it is something I mentioned, or some other parameter, is the lens in which you should look at your work to un-cover whether or not it's the right fit for you.

Jim Collins, in the book "Good to Great", talks about the concept of being on the right bus but maybe in the wrong seat. If you are in a good environ-ment, and being valued, and you're still not happy in your job, it's likely that you are in the wrong seat!

If you are clearly in the right seat, enjoy your environment, have the oppor-tunity to grow, know the importance of your work, and feel fulfillment, then you are in a position to succeed.

The second part of this question was how you feel when you have finished the work day. The ideal way to feel is a sense of satisfaction and a measure of fulfillment. Perhaps a little physically tired, but not worn out emotionally and physically.

Since you will be optimizing your health and relationship circles, you are in a position to complete the work day and go home and fully participate in the other valuable parts of your life. You likely have some measure of a commute, and this is time when you can decompress from the work day and recharge for the next several hours.

This is very difficult if the work completely drains you both physically and emotionally. Reflect again on what I've said here. If all the aspects you've read about line up well, and yet you still feel drained, you are either not in your strength zones enough or there is some type of inefficiency that is causing you to work too much in crisis mode. This may be your inefficiency or it may be a systemic issue in the organization.

Life is too short and uncertain to not be doing work that makes you feel good.

EXCELLING AT WORK

Excellence is a mindset and if you can implement this mindset your workday will become positive and you'll be more successful at work. Use these simple tips to become an outstanding asset to your company.

Be a Go-To Person: Whenever a new opportunity arises for something that needs to be done, volunteer to do it. You may not always be chosen, but your team player attitude will not go unnoticed.

Do More Than You're Paid For: How often have you heard the words "that's not my job" uttered at work? If you're asked to help with something, do it. If you see someone who needs a hand, lend it. If you see trash on the floor, pick it up. Do you have an idea for the company or for your department that can help your job be more impactful? Flesh it out and share it with your boss. Napoleon Hill in his famous book "Think and Grow Rich" talks about this concept. It's powerful.

Over Deliver: When you are tasked with something, do it so well that it will shock the person who asked you. Don't say anything about how well you are going to do it, just do it.

Stay Humble: You never have to tell anyone how good you are. Just do the best you can, all the time, and let your work speak for itself. When you are acknowledged for a job well done, say thank you and share the credit with anyone who helped make it possible.

Invest in Your Own Professional Development: Just a few minutes per day reading, listening to a podcast, or watching a video about your profession and working on your skills will make a massive difference over time. It will begin to show up in your ideas, your actions, and your vocabulary. It will be noticeable to those who are in a position to move you up. It will also grow your confidence which will impact your performance.

Hire a Coach: Coaching is an investment in self that typically leads to significant break-throughs in performance. It's not an overnight fix, it's a process that helps you identify and develop your strengths, uncover your blocks and weaknesses, and pinpoint how you can be more effective.

In Kouzes and Posner's best-selling book "The Leadership Challenge," they say this about coaching:

"No one ever got to be the best at anything without the constructive feedback, probing questions, and active teaching of respected coaches."

If you consider this for a moment you know it's true. Most everyone who strives to be a top performer in their field works with coaches. Having coached many successful business people in my career, I've seen firsthand the power behind this. Working with a coach makes you more accountable to yourself and unlocks the capabilities you may not know you have.

For most of my professional life, my mentors and coaches were books. The closest thing I had to a true mentor was back in my banking days when I worked for a man named Bruce. He saw my potential and invested time in teaching me the work. Not coincidentally, this short window of time was one where I first began to achieve something I felt good about. That ended abruptly when the bank I was working for had a regulatory issue and lost the ability to make loans on real estate, which eliminated the need for my position. I lost my mentor and I had to learn most everything on my own for the next few decades.

It wasn't until I was well into my 50s that I hired my first coach. This is why I am such a fan of purposeful professional development. It makes a big difference, but it is still a lot of trial and error because the implementation is solo. This is why I am so adamant about these two things together, professional development (training) and having a coach. If I had to do it all over again, I would hire a coach immediately and have them direct the professional development.

INCREASING OPPORTUNITIES FOR ADVANCEMENT

The single thing that drives all of your opportunities is your credibility. Credibility is about trust. The more trusted you are, the more opportunities you will receive. It is this simple.

The thing to recognize is that credibility is a perception. You are offered opportunities in life based on your perceived credibility. When you take action on that opportunity, the result will confirm the perceived credibility or prove it was a poor perception.

The cool thing about this perception is that you don't have to exceed expectations. If you just meet the expectation it will automatically lift your perceived credibility and you will soon be trusted with a newer and slightly better opportunity (having said that, I am a fan of over delivering).

If you over deliver, then you have created a significant jump in your credibility and you will be trusted to an even greater level making the next opportunity bigger.

I use the word perceived because it's not really possible to know until the credibility is tested, as to whether it's true.

The beautiful thing about credibility is that you can develop it on purpose. Credibility is simply a combination of your *character* and your *competence* in the area of work. These are things you can work on to grow your credibility which goes hand in hand with your reputation.

"Working with a coach makes you more accountable to yourself and unlocks the capabilities you may not know you have."

CHARACTER & COMPETENCE

You have to work on both. If you are perceived of high character but low competency then you will not have a credibility level worthy of opportunity. If you are perceived of high competency and low character, you will be limited because people either don't like you or can't trust you as a person. Both are vital.

Competency errors can be forgiven. We all make mistakes. Sometimes you will be given a task that you simply have not acquired the full skill set to complete. Instead of trying to fake your way through this, let the person know that there is an area of this task that you will need some assistance on because it falls outside of your current level of skill. Then you will have been honest and likely be provided access to the people or other resources to do the job.

Character mistakes are not easily forgiven or forgotten. If you have made a mistake in the work, admit the mistake and ask for help in how to do better. This shows that you can be trusted to do the right thing. When a mistake is handled properly, it will actually build your character reputation while you are still developing your competence. If you don't own the mistake this has a double negative effect. It shows a lack of competency, and more importantly, it shows a lack of character.

You build character trust by starting with basics, some of which you learned when you were a child. Here is a reminder:

- Treat others with kindness, honesty, and respect. I'm sure you are shocked to see that again, but as the saying goes "repetition is the mother of skill."
- Never make an excuse or blame someone else for your error. Take ownership for your mistakes.
- Always keep your commitments. Commitment is doing the thing you said you would do, regardless of how you feel about it once you've started.
- Be trusting of others. Err on the side of giving someone the benefit of the doubt.
- Be candid. If something is going to be challenging, don't sugar-coat it. Say it like it is.
- Be open-minded. You will never know everything about anything.
- Always keep a confidence. Only one slip of the tongue that betrays a confidence will wipe out any chance for trust with someone. Be a vault.
- If you would not say something to someone's face, don't say it to anyone else.
- Listen to others as if they matter.
- Always give credit to others for the contributions of their work and ideas.
- Be prompt. This sends a signal you can be counted on.
- Don't complain. There will be many times in your work life when things are very difficult. Even if you don't feel positive, be the person that can be counted on to continue to work forward without complaint.
- When you bring a problem to someone, also bring at least a few ideas for how to solve it.

I'm sure you can add other ideas, but this is a solid list that will serve you very well in building a strong trust of character at your workplace.

By being diligent in cultivating both sides of the credibility equation, you will be right at the top of the list for advancement opportunities in both your own workplace and with other organizations.

TAKE THE PRESSURE OFF

One of the biggest things that will cause you sleepless nights and negatively influence your moods is the stress of financial pressure. It's my perspective that most financial pressure is caused by undisciplined behavior that results in overspending and having too little in reserve.

Having lived through my own personal financial crisis in the past, I know how devastating this can be and how it can impact your life. Struggling to meet your financial obligations is a primary factor in living with a scarcity mentality and it greatly limits your choices in life.

We live in an age where credit is readily available. This gives us the opportunity to buy things we truly cannot afford to buy, and do things we shouldn't be doing yet. In other words, it gives us the chance to enjoy the fruits of labor we have not yet performed. And it's a deadly trap.

If you have unsecured debt, like a credit card, make a plan to pay this off as quickly as you can. It will squeeze you a little and you will have to forgo some things you would like to have and do in the short term, but alleviating this underlying stress is important to your health and your relationships.

Credit cards are great to have for convenience, emergencies, and the loyalty programs. However, you need to have a budget so you can pay off the balance each month and avoid the huge interest rates that are part of the credit card system.

Once you have gotten the debt down, pay the entire balance each month, This allows you the convenience of the card, the accumulation of the points to use for a vacation or special purchases, and the details of all your spending for accounting purposes, without any interest payments that eat into your true cash flow.

Next, set aside at least 10% of your income for long term investment purposes so you can take advantage of the compounding impact of interest rates, appreciation, and market gains. If you haven't been doing this already, at first it will feel like it tightens things up because you will have less money to spend. However, the peace of mind you will develop over time will more than make up for it, and after a few months you really won't notice it.

The goal is to create as much financial security as possible. While anything can happen at any moment in life, taking charge of your spending and saving will ease the stress, even if you are tightening your belt for a while to do it. Like exercise, the end result is long term and worth it.

The third thing I suggest is to build a safety net, so to speak. Most financial experts encourage people to have six months of living expenses set aside in readily liquid funds in case of a significant emergency or a job loss. To get started, set aside a portion of your income, again 10% is a good start just for your emergency fund. And remember, it is only for legitimate emergencies.

The reason you want this to be separate from your long-term investments, is that you don't want to be in a position where you have to liquidate your compounding financial assets for a short-term issue. Usually, there are tax implications to doing this, and there could also be penalties, depending on the financial vehicles you are using. The other issue would be the nature of the investment. If the long-term money is in the stock market for example, you don't want to be in a position to have to sell the stock regardless of where the market is.

It's a good idea to seek the advice of a financial advisor to come up with a manageable long-term strategy.

The last thing to address in this section is the reality that job change is a part of life. The average American will have a new job every four years or so. Sometimes this is by choice, but often it's a result of a job loss. The business climate changes rapidly and there is very little security in a job. Currently the pace of change is staggering and it is only going to continue to accelerate. As a result, industries are constantly in flux, as are the companies in them. This means employees are constantly at risk of being affected by change.

Having a safety net affords you the time to make the best choice for you when change happens, instead of having to operate out of fear and take the first thing that is available. One of the smartest things you can do in today's economic climate is create additional income streams for your household so that you are not solely dependent on the income from your job. The best time to do this is when you already have a job that is taking care of your day to day living and building long-term wealth. This way you can work without the pressure of having to earn a lot of money right away and take the time to develop something that makes a major difference in your life. This is commonly called a "side gig" which we'll discuss in the next chapter.

TIME AT WORK

You may have noticed that at no point in this section did I mention that you have to be the first to arrive and the last to leave in your job. There will be times during special circumstances when you have to put in more hours, and you should. That's part of being a team player and a natural part of success.

The key to being successful in your career is productivity, not hours spent. In general, to live the best life possible, you take care of yourself, the people you love, and do an awesome job in your work, and you do it *efficiently*.

Your relationship will not go well if you are consistently over-working. It's expected that you go to work each day, and that is accepted as normal and does not reflect in any way on your relationships. It is when you are consistently spending several more hours per day at work than a normal workday that the relationship will suffer. Your partner in life will likely believe that you care more about your work than you do them.

You simply do not have to overwork to succeed. The key is knowing how to best use your work time to be highly productive. Coming up in Chapter 9, I'll give you the productivity concepts and the keys to managing the other important aspects of your life.

"One of the smartest things you can do in today's economic climate is create additional income streams for your household so that you are not solely dependent on the income from your job."

CHAPTER 8
Heart Pursuit and Side Gig

What is a heart pursuit? It is something that is on your heart to do that refuses to go away. For the purposes of this chapter, a heart pursuit isn't something purely for pleasure or adventure. In other words, let's say you've always wanted to hike the Appalachian Trail or visit Greece. These are more like "bucket list" things, little personal goals that give you something to work toward and are wonderful rewarding experiences when you accomplish them.

A heart pursuit is more like something you have a strong desire to do that requires your time, energy, creativity, and perhaps some risk, and has some measure of deeper meaning for you. Perhaps you have always wanted to paint, or write a book, or play a musical instrument, or start a charity, or start a certain kind of business. The list of possibilities is endless, and unique and personal to each person.

Everyone has something. And I know you do, too.

"You hear people say all the time "When I…then I'll…

If something is on your heart to do the ideal time to start

is now."

Here's why this is so important. It's never going to go away. If you don't do it, there will come a time in your life when you will no longer be able to do it, and depending on the nature of whatever it is, that could come sooner or later. When that time comes, the regret will set in. Regret is an awful feeling that eats at us.

It's likely that if you haven't embarked on doing this heart pursuit thing that has been nagging at you for years it's because you either don't think you have time for it, you don't feel you can afford to do it, or you are simply giving into your fear of trying and failing (for a free audio that may help you with this go to www.toddburrier.com/blog/overcoming-your-four-barriers-to-success).

I had this experience several years ago. I journal almost daily, thereby capturing ideas, thoughts, and of course having a living record of my life. I noticed over time that I was consistently saying to myself in my journals that I should write a book on how to live a balanced life since I had benefited so much from doing so, and the strategies I used had helped many other people.

I had never written a book and had no idea what it would take to do it. After seeing this show up in my journals so many times, I realized it was clearly on my heart to do and that I needed to honor that or I knew I would regret it later. So I simply began. I allocated a little time each day to the project. I didn't do it for profit, I did it because it was on my heart. It took a few years from starting to actually having it published, and it felt incredible to have done it.

You hear people say all the time "When I...then I'll..." Maybe it's "When I have more money," or "When I have more time," or the big one is "When I retire." If you have uttered something like this to yourself about whatever it is that is on your heart to do, here are some perspectives for you.

Conditions will never be perfect. There is rarely a time when you are 100% ready to do something. Life is simply too complex and too uncertain. You will also never truly understand what something is going to take to complete if you have never done it before, so how could you ever plan perfectly?

Life is now. You have no idea how long you have on this planet. If something is on your heart to do the ideal time to start is now. Even if you can only dedicate a few minutes per day, you will have begun. This will have an immediate impact on how you feel. Just starting on this project will lift your spirits. It will require a little discipline and using your time a little differently, and you may have to sacrifice a little of something else to do it, but it will be worth it.

You are congruent with what is in your heart. This may help you a little to deal with the fear aspect. You may not know how to do whatever it is that you are feeling led to, but one thing I know to be true is that our heart is absolutely in line with what we are designed to do. It is our head that gets in the way. If it's in your heart, you can do it. I'm not saying it will be easy or that you won't have a lot to learn, but you can do it. You will realize this later in life when the more mature and experienced version of you looks back in disbelief that the younger version of you didn't take action that was clearly doable! Take the first step and get started.

Now, let's talk specifically about the side gig. If your heart pursuit is something that can generate income, this is obviously ideal. If not, then your side gig can also be looked at as a means to support your heart pursuit, more readily afford your "bucket list," plus creating a safety net through an additional income stream.

The other, and very common, reason for a side gig is a path to working for yourself. If you are not happy with your current job situation, but do not feel you are in a position to make a job change, a career change, or start something of your own full time, then a side gig is the ideal route to take.

To be clear on what a side gig is, if this is a new concept to you, it is anything you do aside from your current job that can create income. It could be a part-time job, a service business that you start on the side on your own, or a home based business where you partner with a company as an independent contractor. Anything from selling real estate, driving an Uber, network marketing, affiliate marketing, referral marketing, cleaning houses, and anything else you could possibly think of could be a side gig.

I am a big fan of starting your own side gig from home because there are many positive impacts on your life from walking this path.

INCOME IMPLICATIONS

A home business impacts your income from two different sides. It allows you to keep more of the money you earn from your career, and it allows you to give yourself a raise.

Keeping more has to do with the tax advantages you gain access to from starting your business. You will have some type of startup cost, though it can be negligible, and these are considered business expenses. A home business is a low investment way to develop an income stream, but it's not a no investment way if you are smart, because in addition to the core business start-up costs it is important to invest in training and/or coaching to help you speed up the learning curve.

Whatever start up materials and training you invest in are tax deductible. You simply have to keep a record of them. The bigger impact from a tax perspective are all the other things you can legitimately begin to turn into business expenses that you previously just spent money on. Things like phone expenses, automotive expenses and mileage, computer expenses, a small portion of your home now becomes a business area, and some meals and entertainment. It's not my intention to give you tax advice because I'm not qualified to do this, but you can do a little research into the tax code and see exactly how to do this easily, or you can go a step further and speak with a tax professional to get full clarity.

The point is that these benefits begin to be applicable immediately once you begin. It is generally worth at least a few hundred dollars per month in a reduction in taxes, meaning you have effectively increased your income.

For this reason alone, it's smart for most people to have some sort of a home business.

The other income aspect is the ability to give yourself a raise by making more money. You can grow your income to whatever size you choose. Be careful though to not get caught up in the idea that you will make a lot of money quickly. While that certainly does happen for some people that is a rarity. You have to look at your business from a realistic lens.

Building a big income through a side gig is a long-term proposition. It takes several years to make a significant amount of money in most self-initiated endeavors, and that's when it's a full-time venture. The key is to be consistent in your work and let the natural evolution of growing a business happen. Ideally you will be able to develop an income of several hundred dollars per month in the first year, grow that into a few thousand per month in the next few years, and take it to another level in the following few years. It depends on your purpose, your desire, and your willingness to work your plan.

You will have to go through a learning curve while at the same time maintaining the other aspects of your life and career. If you work ten hours per week for example, it would take you four years to work what would amount to one year of full-time effort. You have to be patient, diligent, and accepting of the natural ups and downs of growing anything of value.

Having trained and mentored many thousands of people who are home based entrepreneurs over my career, I can say unequivocally that one of the saddest things I have experienced is to see people quit because they didn't have the proper perspective on how long it takes to build a stable business that would provide a substantial income. They get started, learn the basics, begin to become effective, but then fall prey to the desire for instant gratification. This is much more common for the person who is looking to have the side gig become their full-time income than it is for the person working to earn some extra money.

PERSONAL IMPLICATIONS

While income is usually the driver in starting a home business, the impact this will have in the rest of your life is the greatest take away.

I have had a home business for over 30 years. While it has been financially rewarding, what it has done for me as a human being has been incredible, and I've seen the same impact on many others I have mentored.

When you start a business, you are actually undertaking two journeys at the same time. The journey of achieving something and the journey of personal transformation. The skills, both interpersonal and professional, that you learn will have a massive impact on your career as well as your personal life.

The reason this happens is quite simple. Earlier I mentioned that when you begin to grow your competency in any area of your life, this leads to being more confident. When you are more confident, you begin to see the world in a different light. It has a profound effect on your outlook. You see opportunities you would not have seen before.

It grows your self-belief. This impacts how you show up in the world. It is noticeable to others. One example that is relatively fresh is my friend John. John had been working in relatively the same capacity in his company for about 16-17 years. He is a great guy, and was doing okay, but not advancing very much.

"The things and people you treasure most are the ones that have required the most challenge."

He began implementing 3 Circles Living into his life, including starting a side gig, and within 3 years he had two major promotions in his job, and almost doubled his income from his job.

This is a result of the transformation. He always had the raw material, he just became a better version of himself and it was apparent to the people he worked for and it led to his credibility growing which led to new opportunities.

Another additional impact is the uncovering of personal gifts and capabilities. Earlier we explored the idea of strengths. Undertaking a home business venture will stretch you and allow you to see things in yourself that you didn't know before. It's like looking into your tool box and discovering an entire new tray of tools that you didn't realize was in there.

Probably the greatest aspect of transformation comes from the difficulties you face and work through. Building any kind of business will be a struggle most days. Everything of value is. In fact, you can look at your life and you will see the things and people you treasure most are the ones that have required the most challenge. I once heard Ray Higdon say that "if you don't feel like quitting you're not trying hard enough." This is so spot on for what I'm talking about here. It's hard going through the struggles that come with a commitment to accomplish something, it pushes you to your emotional limits. When we make significant commitments in life, we make them while imagining how awesome it will be to attain the thing...not considering how hard it will also be. True commitment is doing it anyway even when it's so tough you don't think you can take another step. Commitment is taking that next step, no matter how difficult.

This builds your character and resiliency. It makes you better able to stand up to the challenges life throws at you. The actual steps of building a business are very simple. It is simply a process of work that you repeat over and over.

It is the mental and emotional component that is making you a better person and changes your perspective.

When you are working at building a business, each day brings a fresh opportunity for something magical to happen. You never know when a single conversation or business activity is going to lead to something great happening for you. You have this possibility every second you are actively engaged.

This potential will be tempered often by disappointment and impatience, which are natural, but as long as you take the next step each day you have unlimited potential for something good to happen.

This is not the day to day experience of someone who is simply stuck doing the same thing and not working at growing themselves or some endeavor.

MONETIZE A HOBBY

When considering your side gig think about something that you love to do and that you have fun doing. You may be able to turn your hobby into an income stream.

Information marketing is an exploding segment of the economy. Whatever the thing is that you love to do...gardening, fishing, sewing, crafting, it doesn't really matter what it is, there is the potential to teach others and earn an income sharing your knowledge.

This is a bit more difficult than just plugging into an existing home business structure, and will have a steeper learning curve and start up process, but it is available as an avenue if you should choose it and there are lots of experts who teach how to do this.

The thing to know is that there are a lot of people who like doing the thing you do who are constantly searching for new insights and information.

BETTING ON YOU

Starting your own venture of some sort is essentially betting on yourself. Taking a risk on you. Most people don't think having a job is risky. Earlier we talked a bit about the reality of today's job. It is simply not very secure, and it's becoming less secure in general.

When you have a job, you are essentially betting on someone else. You are putting your eggs in a basket you don't hold. Jobs are a good thing and I'm not suggesting you shouldn't have one or do the best you can. What I am saying is that you should also be betting on you.

What is your dream? Whatever it is, working for someone else, is only going to play part of a role in helping you accomplish it, unless it has huge income potential. It makes perfect sense when you think of it this way; when you work for someone else, you are applying your skills and talents to helping them build their dream.

Shouldn't you at least do the same thing for your dreams? Life is risky anyway. There is nothing guaranteed. However, working towards what you truly want out of life will guarantee a more exciting and fulfilling journey.

It's never too late to start. Don't worry about what someone else will think. Don't worry about what someone will say. Don't worry about failing.

Just start something and don't stop. It will be a transformation that will change your life and it will trickle down positively onto everyone you love.

CHAPTER 9
How to Make it
All Happen

Now it's time to wrap things up by giving you a roadmap for how to accomplish all the great stuff you are about to implement.

You are now going to get a planning strategy for taking care of your health, your relationships, your career, and your side gig (if you have one), so that you can thrive in all areas.

This will not happen without a plan. Most people have a plan in their work. They have to because it's the only way to ensure that the right things get done at the right time. However, you should also have an over-arching plan for your life with your work being one element in the grand plan.

I teach planning in corporate settings and it's normal to have people admit that they plan at work, but not outside of it. This is no surprise. Planning is not a skill that most people are ever taught. Yet, it is one of the most important personal productivity skills available and one of the easiest to learn and implement. In my first book "Live Full, Live Well" there is a substantial amount of information about planning that will take you through every nuance of defining roles and planning in a detailed and extremely effective manner. If you want to master this skill that would be an excellent resource for you as it has a complete blueprint.

The old adage "if you fail to plan, you plan to fail" is spot on. Since you want to succeed the 3 Circles way and maximize your quality of life, you'll get a simple way to get started here.

STEP ONE - PRIORITIZING

Before you plan, it has to be clear what is important in your life to do relative to what matters most. Your priorities have to drive your planning to make sure you are planning the most important things. Think of it this way, would you rather spend your time fighting fires that you have unknowingly lit or building something solid that makes your life more enjoyable?

This is the difference between being proactive in your priorities or reactive in your priorities. Any time you are being reactive in a priority, which by definition is something important, it typically means something bad is going on. The first few chapters where I talked about health and relationship issues coming up as a result of neglect are examples of this kind of reaction impact.

When you take the proactive approach you will rarely have fires in your areas of priority, and when they arise, it will usually be from something happening you had no control over. That's called "life happening." It happens to everyone. You will never be free of crisis in life, but you can greatly reduce the amount and its impact.

When you plan your daily priorities you avoid neglect which is the mother of all self-inflicted crisis. First you have to identify all your priorities.

For the purposes of 3 Circles Living, you would automatically include health, love relationships, and career/side gig if you have one. Are there other priorities for you that fall outside of these? If so, you need to be clear as to what these are, because you will need to account for them in your planning.

STEP TWO - IDENTIFY THE TASKS & ACTIVITIES TO SUPPORT PRIORITIES

Each priority has a set of basic tasks and activities that must be acted upon consistently to thrive. In the Health Circle, you have things like exercise, personal development, and journaling among other things.

In the Relationship Circle you have specific activities, and focused time investment.

In the Money Circle your work has tasks and activities that need to be performed consistently, and ideally, professional development. The heart pursuit/side gig will also have a set of activities and necessary time investment to move it forward.

Anything else you have established as a priority will also have tasks, activities, and some necessary investment of time.

Take some time and identify what these things are for you so that you are able to account for them in your planning.

STEP THREE - PLANNING BASICS

Once you have identified what you need to be doing to make everything happen, it is now just a function of planning them into your day to be as efficient as possible and to make sure nothing slips through the cracks.

The first thing you need is a planning tool. This can be as simple as an app on your phone, a program on your computer, or if you are old school like yours truly, a physical planner that has dates and pages where you write it all down.

Whatever you use, it has to be easily accessible to you at all times. It should go everywhere you do at least during the work week.

In this planner you need to account for everything. Don't begin a day until it is planned. This rule of thumb will make a huge difference for you. Once the day is started you will be too engaged in what is around you and reacting and interacting and it will be much harder to create a plan.

You have to put everything in the planner including any tasks and appointments. If you don't, not only will you likely forget, but you will not be able to see the planning efficiencies that present themselves when you have a complete picture.

Just 10-15 minutes of daily planning will afford you at least an hour of efficiency. This means it will feel like you have more time, because you will be able to accomplish more. You cannot get more physical time. We all have 24 hours each day. There is no more and no less time, you can only improve your ability to use time in a better way.

"Just 10-15 minutes of daily planning will afford you at least an hour in efficiency."

It's incredible how much more you can accomplish in less time when you plan. When you can see the entire picture you can see opportunities for consolidating things, collaborating with others, delegating to others, and multi-tasking.

For example, whenever you make a trip out of the house consult your planner and take care of everything that can possibly be done in one trip. This results in added efficiency. Consider a phone call you might be able to accomplish at the same time. Simple things with huge time return.

Building efficiency through planning has been helpful for me in the Health Circle. I ride a stationary exercise bike six days per week as part of my physical health strategy. I also do personal and professional development reading daily. Each one of these things is a minimum of 30 minutes of time. If I did one and then the other, then it would take an hour. Instead, I read while I ride. This effectively frees up 30 minutes because both are accomplished at once.

A career and side gig nugget lays in this strategy as well. For example, there are times in the day when it is much more efficient to reach people in business. Plan your day such that you are engaging people directly during these peak times. Each business has its own rhythm so I can't tell you when the best time for yours will be, but you will know within a few minutes of assessing this. In a peak time you may be able to talk to eight people in an hour. In an off peak time you may only be able to talk to four. By working in a peak time, you are able to allocate another hour somewhere else. Only planning reveals this opportunity.

Create the habit of planning. The two best ways to plan are the end of the day for the next day or at the very beginning of your day. I am a morning planner. I know that my brain is the most active early because that is simply my personal rhythm. If you're a night owl, plan then and if you are an early bird do it in the morning.

Pick an environment that is ideal for you to be uninterrupted for this activity and ideally in a spot you enjoy. In the first few weeks you do this, pick the same time and the same place until you have established the habit. At first it may take you ten or fifteen minutes to do a thorough job, but once you have developed the habit, you may be able to do your planning in 5 minutes. This will be an incredibly productive small chunk of time because it will make your days flow and you will be able to easily move from activity to activity.

It really is extraordinary how much you can accomplish when you plan. Melanie laughs at me frequently because my brain has become so hard-wired to use time efficiently. We can be driving to the store and I will be telling her to go a different way because it's 10 seconds faster! I am absolutely horrible at organizing things, but I use time more efficiently than anyone else I know. I was such an undisciplined person as a young man that I had a hard time just paying my bills on time. Cultivating the discipline of planning, led to becoming a master in how I use time.

I typically work on many projects at once, work with several people/clients at once, do all the health and relationship activities I've mentioned, and still have plenty of time to fish, crab, read good books, play with the dogs, and all with very little stress about time.

There's another huge benefit to this relative to personal and professional credibility. When you are a daily planner it's easy to keep commitments and do whatever it is you say you will do. When someone isn't a planner, occasionally they will forget to follow through with something they said they would do. The parties affected by this lack of follow through won't know that you lacked planning skills, they will think you can't be trusted. It is a competency that reflects to the world as a character thing.

STEP FOUR - EXECUTING THE PLAN

Once you have your plan, work it. Your plan will have everything that is important to do in the day. This eliminates the need to think about what to do next. You will certainly have things that pop up that require time you weren't planning for, so make sure that you do not schedule so tightly that you are completely inflexible.

Anything that arises that needs to be addressed should be noted in your planner so you can build it into your future planning. Use the calendar in your planner to help you forward plan. For example, if during a conversation today, a new meeting time is set for the future, or a new project is created, just move forward in your planner and set the meeting in the appropriate time or set a date when to begin working on the project.

Your planner is the key tool to getting your 3 Circles Lifestyle accomplished and achieving much higher levels of productivity in everything that is important to you. The more you execute your comprehensive plan day in and day out, the less stress you will have, the more of what's important you will accomplish, and the higher your quality of life will be.

I realize that I only brushed planning in the most basic way. You can study planning and refine it as much as you want, but simply operating with these few tenets will make a big difference.

CHAPTER 10
Living in the
Sweet Spot

The sweet spot is that special place where all the circles come together and you are thriving in all areas that are of importance to you. This is the spot where you are living your richest life. You are healthy and energized, thriving in your relationships, showing up as your best self in your work, and making your contribution to the betterment of everything you are investing yourself in.

It's an awesome place to live. This is the destination of the road map of this book. But it's not a perfect place to live.

You are still going to have struggle and challenge in your life. You're going to have things that broadside you and throw your life out of whack. You are going to have new journeys that will require you to grow and of course, that means struggle too.

An awesome life is not a life free from heartache or difficulty. These things are part of a well-lived life.

There are a few final things to touch on here.

BE PATIENT

Just because you have read this book, and have begun to shift the order of things and implemented some of the teachings doesn't mean things are instantly going to be wonderful.

It takes time for positive change to really take root and begin to show up in results. There is always a lag between action and visible result. For example, when you first start an exercise program and go do a work out, do you see it right away in your body?

Of course not. You might go two or three weeks before you see any visible difference at all. This is true in all areas of life.

You have to put in the effort first and then you begin to see some result. This is a challenge I know. We want to see results right now!

We are not born as patient creatures. Think about babies. How patient are babies when they're hungry? Do they just happily lay there until someone decides to provide some food? No. They scream until they get food.

That is our nature. As we mature, we become patiently impatient. We are never going to be truly patient, so we simply feel the impatience and then exercise the patience to continue on while we are impatient.

You will have to be patient with multiple things. You will have to be patient with results. They will just never come as fast as you want in the big picture, but you will see noticeable things relatively quickly. When you do see these small results at the beginning, relish those little victories. They show you that you are on the right track.

You will have to be patient with others who are not on the same page with how you have decided to live your life. Just because you have made a decision to shift around your priorities, and go after achieving your richest life possible, they will not automatically know that is what you have done (although at some point you might explain it to them…which I'll talk about in a minute). There will be times when you say "no" to them or other things that don't fit your priorities and planning, be patient with them when they don't understand why.

You will also need to be patient with yourself relative to your growth. Just from what I shared in this book, the things to do to strengthen relationships for example, it will take some time to develop new skills and habits. You are going to make mistakes as you learn. That's okay. It's a normal part of the learning process. I've been teaching people skills for many years and I still make mistakes all the time.

REMIND YOURSELF WHY

As you go forward and things improve for you in all the areas that matter, it can become pretty easy to become complacent and have old habits creep back in.

Human beings are quite resilient and as part of that resiliency, we don't typically remember the full extent of the pain we have experienced in the past. Think about something physical or emotional that was incredibly painful to you in the past. When you think about it now, you know it was painful, but can you really feel just how painful it was at the time? No. Time heals. Maybe not fully, but enough to go forward.

This is one of the reasons people who have endured a lot of hardship in their life, have an easier time navigating challenge… they have gotten thicker skin so to speak.

The point here is that the 3 Circles Living needs to become an immovable platform that you operate from. Once you have it all working well and you are experiencing the positive results it brings, you will naturally forget why it was so important to follow this routinely.

This is when you can start giving into the "I don't feel like it today" issue. The easiest place for this to start is the health circle. Once it starts there, then naturally the impact of letting down is going to go to the relationship circle and then into the money circle.

For me, I simply think about Melanie. It's that easy. I remind myself when I don't feel like doing my health thing, that this isn't just for me. It's also for her.

PAY IT FORWARD

As you begin to get into the sweet spot, the difference in your life is going to be more and more noticeable to the people around you.

Healthy, vibrant, joyful people give off a magnetic energy. The people you are consistently around will see this and likely say something.

The people you do business with, whether it's co-workers, employees, leadership, vendors, or clients, are going to notice this too. Not just in observing you, but also seeing the positive impact you are having on the people you are in touch with.

This will be true when you are out and about in your community as well.

Share what you have learned with them. All around you are people struggling to figure it all out. Many of them are feeling a little hopeless. Be a light for them.

You cannot change anyone. You can, however, be a catalyst for someone to change, and then be a supporter and encourager as they work at changing.

We are never going to live in a perfect world. But imagine how different the world might be if everyone was healthier, more joyful, making their best contribution, treating others with kindness, honesty, and respect, and doing many of the other things talked about in the pages of this book.

Call me crazy, but I believe that when we know something that can help someone, we have a responsibility to share. Perhaps if we each just help one person to achieve their richest life possible, and they in turn help one person…who knows, maybe we can make the world a better place.

Steve Jobs famously said "Here's to the crazy ones, the misfits, the rebels, the troublemakers, the round pegs in the square holes... the ones who see things differently -- they're not fond of rules... You can quote them, disagree with them, glorify or vilify them, but the only thing you can't do is ignore them because they change things... they push the human race forward, and while some may see them as the crazy ones, we see genius, because the ones who are crazy enough to think that they can change the world, are the ones who do."

It starts with you. Are you ready to live your richest life possible? If so, you have flipped the script. Shifted your perspective on the order of what's important and started down the path to a more fulfilling life. Who's life might be changed forever just because you made a new choice? The possibilities are endless.

Some Final Words

THERE ARE A NUMBER OF WAYS YOU CAN CONNECT WITH ME IF YOU WISH.

I steadily write and share new content that will serve you in all aspects of the 3 Circles via my blog. You can subscribe to that here: https://toddburrier.com/blog/subscribe/

You will not get piles of emails from me, likely one or two per week as a normal course of things, and I do not make your contact information available to anyone else.

You can also follow me on my Facebook Fan Page: https://www.facebook.com/toddburrier.page

I do some live video, inspirational posts, and other content that is centered on personal and professional development.

Another place you can find me is on Youtube at: https://www.youtube.com/user/ToddBurrier

Also you can connect with me on Linkedin: https://www.linkedin.com/in/toddburrier/

I do much deeper training on many of the topics I shared in the book. If you would like to have me speak at a Company Retreat, provide a keynote, or do a workshop on site or online contact me here: https://toddburrier.com/contact/ and we can discuss it.

If you are in the home business industry, there are many resources that I've produced specifically for you that are available at: https://toddburrier.com/products/

And finally, if this book has truly touched you to the point you would like to write a recommendation on Amazon or Linkedin, or anywhere else, don't be shy, that might end up being the tiny nudge that helps someone else take the step to change their life.

Thank you again for allowing me to serve you in your journey to achieve your richest life possible.

Many Blessings, Todd Burrier

I'm grateful that you opened this book and stayed with me until the end.

But this isn't the end.

It's the beginning of an entirely new chapter in your life. I hope you will reach out to me and share your story of change as you work to achieve your richest life possible.

Acknowledgements

This book doesn't happen without the support and encouragement of my wife Melanie. Not only did she urge me to put this on paper, but she oversaw the details. If it weren't for her, this is still at best floating around in a word file, or worse, in my head. Not only is she a beautiful person inside and out, she is my soul mate and has been the one person who has always believed in me. Thank you for everything my love.

For Jane Maulucci (www.thereactivevoice.com). Jane is very talented and knowledgeable about writing in general and helped greatly by clarifying the many facets of this project. She also edited and provided guidance throughout. Thank you Jane, for your patience and attention to detail.

For my longtime friend Dave Ryner (www.echoechocom.com). From where I'm standing, Dave is a creative genius. He did an awesome job of taking something I said and turned it into something visually powerful. He created all of the graphics, did the formatting, and handled the details for getting the book print ready. Thank you for everything my friend.

Notes

Notes

Notes

Notes

Notes

Notes

Made in the USA
Columbia, SC
15 July 2020